Prai

MW00780083

"I was very impressed. The book is a thoughtful and timely work covering one of the most crucial issues facing policing."
—Charles Ramsey, CNN contributor and former
Commissioner of the Philadelphia Police Department

"Ross's over forty years of law enforcement experience and research provided him an opportunity to become an expert in the area of ethics-based policing. His principles of accountability create a foundation that ensures officers and officials provide police service in a fair, equitable, and consistent manner. . . . A must read for all police executives, managers, recruiters, and trainers."
—Al Broadbent, former Director of Security,
US Department of Commerce, and former Vice President
of Police and Security, Amtrak

"Ross Swope has written the seminal book on police ethics and presents, explains, and shows how a police culture influences police performance that can be good or not so good. . . . A clear guide to police and sheriff departments and other law enforcement organizations for strengthening an ethical culture and reducing or eliminating the use of excessive force."
—William P. McManus, Chief of Police, San Antonio,
Texas, and former Chief of Police, Minneapolis, Minnesota

"Impressive, timely, and on point. *Ethics-Based Policing* text focuses on the building blocks of integrity and how to implement and strengthen police integrity, resulting in a reduction or elimination of use of excessive force, improved police performance, and a strong bond between communities and the police. Profound!"
—Victor Brito, Chief of Police, Rockville, Maryland

"I have had the privilege of working with Ross for over twenty-five years. In his various assignments, he has been relentless in demanding ethical behavior from his subordinates and coworkers. He is very well positioned to expound on the importance of ethics-based policing in his book."

—Robert C. White, former Chief of Police, Denver,
Colorado, and former Chief of Police, Louisville, Kentucky

"Building trust with the communities we serve is not a new issue, but undeniably a seminal one in policing today. There are no magic solutions. . . . Ross provides a compelling discussion, including key building blocks to help address the most pressing problems facing law enforcement."

—Kim C. Dine, former Chief of the United States Capitol
Police and former Chief of Police, Frederick, Maryland

ETHICS-BASED POLICING

SOLVING THE USE OF EXCESSIVE FORCE

ROSS SWOPE

EDEN WOOD PUBLISHING
Gambrills, Maryland

Eden Wood Publishing
Gambrills, Maryland 21054
edenwoodpublishing@gmail.com

Printed in the United States of America
28 27 26 25 24 23   1 2 3 4 5 6 7 8

Cover photograph: National Journal © 2012 National Journal Group LLC
Cover and book design: Sandra Jonas

Publisher's Cataloging-in-Publication Data

Names: Swope, Ross E., 1950–, author.
Title: Ethics-Based Policing: Solving the Use of Excessive Force / Ross E.
    Swope.
Description: Gambrills, Maryland : Eden Wood Publishing, 2023. | Includes
    bibliographical references and index.
Identifiers: LCCN 2022923034 | ISBN 9798986993812
Subjects: LCSH: Police ethics. | Law enforcement — Moral and ethical aspects
    — United States. | Police-community relations — United States. | BISAC:
    SOCIAL SCIENCE / Criminology.
Classification: LCC HV7924 .S96 | DDC 174.936320973
LC record available at http://lccn.loc.gov/2022923034

To the thousands of men and women
who have sworn to protect and serve
and perform their duties with dedication,
sacrifice, commitment, and integrity

CONTENTS

FOREWORD

For more than twenty years, I had the opportunity to work with and learn from Ross Swope, as his subordinate, colleague, student, and friend. Throughout our respective careers, we worked together on various assignments. His experiences and knowledge are impressive and rare.

You see, Ross is the only commander who served his career with the Washington, DC, police in line assignments. That means for twenty-seven years, he was out on the street with those under his charge to serve the public around the clock in every social-economic neighborhood in the city. When I was invited to become the chief of police in Washington, DC, in 2007, I knew where to turn for candid, trusted and sage discussions, and Ross was there to help me.

I first heard one of his lectures about accountability and responsibility as the foundation of police ethics when I was a young police commander and a master's student at Johns Hopkins University. I have applied his principles of ethics-based policing throughout my thirty-year career with the police force in Washington, DC, which included serving as the chief of police for nearly ten of those years. I have seen firsthand the impact that ethics-based policing has on law enforcement and the communities they protect and serve. This approach builds and strengthens the bond between the police and communities, a bond that is so necessary for effective service.

Police reform has dominated headlines and political agendas for nearly a decade, and yet there seems to be no clear path to success for those responsible for leading the transformation—until now. Through the lens of an accomplished police leader and Fulbright Scholar, *Ethics-Based Policing: Solving the Use of Excessive Force* examines the crucial role that ethics play in today's discussion of police reform and the policing profession.

Police departments have policies, procedures, and orders concerning unethical conduct. So why is it that a few officers who engage in conduct unbecoming still manage to tarnish the shields worn by so many? Ross reviews the history of misconduct, why it is taking place, who can correct it, and how. It *can* be fixed. Circumstances can improve. It does not require time-consuming legislation. It does not require media impute or advice from those who have little experience in the profession of policing.

Ethics-Based Policing delves into the fundamental issues of police misconduct—the use of excessive force in particular—and it explores the role leadership plays in creating an ethical culture. Doing so will effectively change the challenging circumstances the police profession now finds itself.

This book explores the essential role that first-line supervisors and mid-level managers play in creating an ethical culture. As Ross so aptly states, it is they, the last leaders to touch the mail, the ones responsible for the performance of officers, who must step up. When these first-line supervisors, sergeants, and corporals, along with mid-level managers, lieutenants, and captains, fail in their responsibility to hold subordinates accountable for their conduct, bad things happen. The use of excessive force will continue unabated until a strong ethical culture is instilled by these police officials.

An ethical culture is about consequences and rewards and the effects these actions have on a unit or a department. Consequences must be in place for those who engage in brutality and other unethical behavior, and rewards for those whose performance of duty is highly ethical. "Highly ethical" means they practice what Ross describes as the police core virtues: prudence, trust, courage, intellectual honesty, justice, self-effacement of interests, and responsibility. The actions of first-line supervisors and mid-level managers—or the lack there of—profoundly influences how the officers under their span of control will perform, and officer performance is based on the culture created by those same police officials.

The book's approach is both interesting and informative. It describes a theory, such as the Police Core Virtue Bell Curve, and then provides real-life examples to illustrate how applying that theory works. The book also walks the reader through a brief history of police misconduct and recommends a path to achieving and building an ethical culture.

In 1996, the Department of Justice convened the National Symposium on Police Integrity in Washington, DC, a three-day meeting with two hundred participants. The author was one of only two police officers invited to give a keynote speech. All the speeches presented at the symposium were published in 1997 and included the thoughts and observations of many national leaders, including Attorney General Janet Reno.

Following the publication, the Los Angeles Police Department (LAPD) was rocked by the Rampart Area Corruption Incident, which received national attention. A major report was prepared and published in 2000. In that report, they wrote about the book of symposium speeches. "Though there are a number of interesting and insightful viewpoints expressed in that publication, there is one in particular which is most relevant to the issues at hand. That observation came from Captain Ross Swope, Metropolitan Police Department, Washington, DC."

In short, the author's published speech laid out what the LAPD found to be the major cause of corruption: the failure to hold officers accountable.

Ross Swope has been published over thirty times in academic and practitioner publications nationally, including *The Police Chief, Law and Order Magazine, United States Attorney Bulletin*, and internationally in *Police Review* (UK), *La tribune du commissaire de police* (France), *Interopol* magazine (France), and *Crime Prevention–International Experiences* (Germany).

In addition to being an adjunct professor at Johns Hopkins, he has published work that has been used at the Federal Law Enforcement Training Academy, police academies across the country, and at many universities.

Following a successful forty-three-year career in policing, three master's degrees, and many publications on policing, the author was struck by the current state of policing. After giving so much to his profession, he refused to sit by. He applied his usual dedication and commitment to create this book.

I highly recommend *Ethics-Based Policing* to anyone playing a role in shaping the police reform effort in our country, and I endorse it as a must-read for law enforcement leaders at all levels, members of the media, and legislators involved in these efforts.

Cathy L. Lanier
Chief of the Metropolitan Police Department
Washington, DC (Retired)

ON BECOMING A COP

My father was a cop. As far back as my memory goes, I was surrounded by honorable, dedicated, fine men of courage who also carried a badge. Along with my parents and brother, these men and their families, most of whom had children my age, became my community.

In those days in that community, the color of one's skin was of no consequence. In solidarity, social gatherings included everyone—and we socialized regularly. Shrimp feasts were a monthly occurrence, taking place first in one family's home, then another. As a child and later as a teen, I looked forward to these grand events as much as anyone, except that I didn't fancy shrimp in those days. As a teen, I often visited the station house and even became best friends with some of Dad's friends despite the age difference.

My father didn't plan on becoming a cop. He was drafted into the army during World War II. Upon discharge, he expected to return to his pre-war job, but the company he had worked for wouldn't take him back, even though they were supposed to. So my father turned to policing. In 1947, he took the oath to serve and protect with the Metropolitan Police Department in Washington, DC. In those days, starting pay was around $2,000 a year for a six-day work week, not including any court appearances he might have to make when he was off duty. He received no compensation for that.

I grew up ten miles outside of Washington, DC, in Prince Georges County, Maryland. The location was problematic. Most of the kids I played with dropped out of high school, suffered drug addiction, and went to prison. Many died young. Two young men who lived on the same street as I did committed felony crimes and were shot by the police. I don't believe any of these young people had the same opportunity I had to stand in the shadows of men of conviction, courage, empathy, and sacrifice—men who cared.

Some of the cops I knew hunted for birds and game, but my dad did not. He did, however, buy me a military surplus .22 caliber rifle when I was young and took me to a National Rifle Association training course. I was hooked.

Dad's police friends found out I enjoyed shooting, so when I became a teenager, they often invited me to join their hunting expeditions. For decades, I spent days and weeks at a time in the woods with them. They taught me excellent hunting and shooting skills, but even more valuable were the life lessons I garnered through their actions, dispositions, and words of wisdom.

Stuart Heflin stands out in particular. As my father's police partner for many years, he and Dad were close. We grew close too. Even though he wasn't a blood relative, my brother and I always called him Uncle Stuart. Next to my father, Uncle Stuart was the finest man I have ever had the privilege of calling a friend, mentor, and hunting partner. He was quick to laugh, light-hearted, kind, a fine shot, and he could spin a yarn with the best of them.

I visited several of my father's friends as they recovered from various injuries over the years. Uncle Stuart was one of them. A number of years ago, a felon fleeing in a car intentionally struck him down. To this day I remember him lying in his bed at home with bandages tightly bound around his chest. He recovered from that injury, thankfully. I gave his eulogy when he passed away five years ago at the age of ninety-five.

My father was injured on the job several times. The worst injury occurred when I was an infant. One evening while on duty and in uniform, he witnessed a group of drunken soldiers on leave in Washington, DC, attack another man. Never one to stand by, Dad entered the melee without hesitation. The beating he received sent him to the hospital. From that day forward, he wore a back brace. Throughout my childhood, I saw Dad stuck in bed for a week at a time, lying on a heating pad because his back had slipped out. Surgeries failed to correct the injuries he received while protecting someone he never knew.

Despite their experiences, my father and the men he worked with didn't grow hard. They weren't prone to violence. They loved their families, their careers, and life in general. They were men I liked to be around. They seldom talked about the job. They seldom passed advice to me, but when it was given, I soaked it up.

Words don't hurt.
Serve those most in need first.
Anger serves no purpose and will cause you trouble.
Treat everyone with dignity and respect; it is too easy not to.

Those words reflected the way these men conducted themselves. They never seemed disturbed, despite what they encountered. They were kind, friendly, and generous to others, upbeat and happy, and they always wore smiles.

Dad taught me all about kindness and generosity. When I was about ten years old, my chores earned me ten cents a week for allowance. One Saturday, Dad came home from work and told me about a man he had met that day, a man who had no place to live and very little to eat. Dad pointed out that we were lucky while that poor man had fallen on hard times.

"Ross," he said, "would you like to give that man a dollar?"

A dollar was ten weeks' worth of allowance. I had a dollar because I'd saved it. Dad applied no pressure. His question wasn't a demand in any way. He had simply shared a story about his day and posed a question to me. I had never seen a homeless person, nor had I experienced any kind of deprivation. At the time, I assumed Dad had already given that man some of his own hard-earned money. As I thought about that, it occurred to me that he did it as a form of service, and it made him feel good.

That's all it took. I gave that man a dollar and never forgot how good it made me feel. That message was continually reinforced. In forty-three years of police service, I saw countless acts of generosity and effacement of self interest performed by those I worked with.

These qualities were second-nature to Dad, and others noticed.

My father was an on duty as a uniformed patrolman on March 1, 1954, when four armed members of the Puerto Rican Nationalist Party entered the US Capitol and fired onto the floor of the House Chambers. Three men were immediately captured, but one, Irvin Flores (Rodriguez), escaped.

Information about the incident streamed over the police radio. Dad reacted quickly. He knew that after committing a crime, offenders attempt to get as far away from the scene as possible. Out-of-town bus terminals were on his beat, so he began searching for the gunman. Although he found and arrested Flores, credit for the arrest went to the detectives who took the over the case. However, his initiative was rewarded with an opportunity to become a "plainclothesman," where he remained until his retirement.

That assignment made my mother happy; the role exposed him to much less danger.

The solidarity established between my father and his friends on the job didn't dissipate when they left policing, so my exposure to these good men continued. Even during my college years, after Dad had retired, I attended gatherings with them. These men made a difference in others lives—they helped, they saved, they protected, and they served. I wanted to be one of them. I also wanted to be one of the best.

Following graduation from high school, I matriculated to the University of Maryland at College Park, Maryland, where I took many police courses as electives. I received a bachelor's degree in Business Administration in 1972. After working my way through college at a desk job, I knew I didn't want to spend my life behind a desk.

As I considered my future, the lives of my father and his colleagues were ever present, nudging me toward a decision. Although I knew my folks had no desire for me to enter law enforcement, so much historical interaction with cops was a powerful driver. I had to follow my own path. In 1973, I applied to the DC Police and was sworn in as one of only ten officers with a college degree in a force of nearly five thousand.

My mother broke down and wept. "You are the first family member to graduate from college," she begged. "Please don't go, Ross."

I took her hand. "I understand, but this is something I have to do, Mom."

Dad never said a word to me one way or the other, but shortly after being sworn in, I learned he was spreading the word about my position. He was proud of my role as a DC policeman but could never say that to Mom.

My brother had it much easier when he joined the ranks a few years later. Apparently, I wasn't the only one influenced by the men we spent so much time with. My mother eventually accepted my career choice and, in fact, became proud of me. I heard it in her voice and saw it in her eyes as she introduced me to others over the years:

"He is with the DC police."
"He is a sergeant with the DC police."
"He is a lieutenant with the DC police."
"He is a captain with the DC police."

Graduating from the police academy at the top of my class afforded me the opportunity to select my assignment. I chose the Third District, a very busy area even though it was the smallest. On the Saturday night following my Friday graduation, I worked the midnight tour. I had Tuesdays and Wednesdays off with shifts that rotated every two weeks between daywork, evenings, and midnights. I chose those shifts to learn as much as possible in a short period of time. I wanted the experience to become skilled, competent, confident, and successful in my goal—to make a difference in the service of those who needed it the most.

The role was not all peaches and cream. Not all sergeants behaved like enlightened leaders. One of them challenged me with his first words: "What are you doing here, 'college boy'?" This short-statured man was short fused too, eager to display his authority, and only showed his favorites any kind of common courtesy. I never saw him on the street or heard him on the radio like all the other sergeants.

My first lesson on how not to lead.

Anyway, the nickname stuck.

I kept my mouth shut and did my job, but I was tested, that's for sure! I was frequently assigned the most dangerous drug and crime beats in the city, often walking the foot patrol alone with only one method of contacting the station house: the police call box. Every five or six blocks throughout the city, a locked metal box holding a telephone stood on a cast-iron base. The telephone connected directly to a switchboard in every station house. Within a year, officers on foot patrol were issued one-way radios.

I came to know the neighborhood well and often arrived on the scene of a crime before the dispatched patrol car appeared. I did whatever seemed logical and appropriate. Apparently, my behaviors were often unexpected. At the scene of a 2 a.m. house fire, I stood in the pouring rain directing traffic. When more police arrived, a congenial sergeant approached me. "Hey, college boy," he said, "get in the car."

As I obliged, glad to get out of the rain, he turned on his overhead lights. We sat in the car and talked until the fire department cleared the scene. Then he took me for coffee at a late-night diner.

When I had eighteen months under my belt, an investigative position became available. As I filled out the application, the sergeant who had assigned my nickname came up behind me. "Hey, college boy. Do that on your own time. Hit the street. NOW."

I got the investigative position. Two years later, I was promoted to the grade of detective. From there, it was onward and upward with much work to accomplish. Over the years, I worked in every part of the city, leading both uniformed officers and those in investigative positions, but eventually I found my way home to the Third District. I became its commander with nearly five hundred officers assigned.

From the day I walked my first foot beat on a male-only force to the time I retired and women assumed roles of equal responsibility and valor, I lived by one mantra. This mantra was cultivated by the men who guided me through my formative years, most of all my father. That mantra is a question that remains with me to this day: What would I do if my mom, dad, brother, other family member, or friend faced the tragedies I saw so many times?

The answer remains the same too. I would not walk away. I would protect and serve them with dedication and sacrifice, just as I would my family. Sadly, most of the time, people experiencing the worst need have nowhere else to turn but the police. When I was a member of the force, neither I nor the men and women under my charge would fail them.

It is my intention to help realign the role of policing with the community relationships and values that I witnessed growing up, relationships based on the police core virtues of prudence, truth, courage, justice honesty, and effacement of self-interest and responsibility.

INTRODUCTION

The Time for Change Is Now

The police profession I so faithfully served for over four decades is tarnished. We've all seen media reports about a few officers committing shameful, criminal acts in the performance of their sworn duties. Use of excessive force has painted all police officers with a broad brush of dishonor, ultimately rocking the fundamental integrity of policing while harming citizens and good police officers alike. I am disheartened and disturbed that a few corrupt police officers can inflict so much damage. We may or we may not agree on the statistics involved, but one thing we can all agree on is this: some police officers use excessive force, and something must be done to end that behavior. Now.

Despite the current circumstances, I believe policing is still an honorable profession. What could be more worthy than to protect, serve, keep the peace, and uphold the Constitution of the United States? I brought many years of university study in justice and behavioral science into my role as a leader in the police force. In forty-three years on the job, I worked with thousands of officers and police officials who performed their duty with honor, along with care, compassion, sacrifice, courage, dedication, commitment, and empathy.

Today, these dedicated professionals are threatened by the actions of a few corrupt members of the force. For them, for the many hundreds of thousands of honorable police officers and detectives across the nation, for the communities I bonded with, and for other disheartened communities, I am compelled to write this book and draw from my experience to share a proven, workable solution.

While this book is directed specifically toward policing, these principles address similar stories being played out in other law enforcement organizations at the federal and state level. They address the lack of consistent application of ethical leadership in organizations and agencies of all stripes and need to be applied in many fields that provide service to the public. Social services like Adults in Need of Supervision, Child Protective Services, and Code Enforcement are just a few agencies where I've seen the ball dropped. Because ethical leadership was lacking, bad things happened.

Many voices beyond law enforcement are calling for changes to the ways police conduct their business. Academics, sociologists, news reporters, and social media posts all have opinions, suggestions, solutions, and demands. Unfortunately, many of these contributors have never had their feet on the ground. They've never engaged in police work. They're so far removed from its realities that they don't understand the complications implied by their demands. They don't know what they don't know.

ABC News, in part, recommends that applicants be tested for every conceivable tendency, ranging from bias and aggression level to empathy and impulse control, along with a background test.[1] Sounds good, so where do we find a battery of tests such as these with empirically proven reliability and validity? Years in the future, if they are ever developed. Psychological testing is already in the forefront of recruitment. In an article for the Balance Careers, Timothy Roufa writes, "It's estimated that more than 90% of law enforcement agencies in the U. S. require psychological screening of their applicants, either before or after receiving a conditional offer of employment."[2]

Dr. Gary Fischler, an assistant professor of psychology at the University of Minnesota and a forensic psychologist whose practice specializes in the evaluation of potential law enforcement officers describes extensive screening—general intelligence; judgment; the ability to perform boring or tedious tasks, tolerate stress, and deal with supervision; reasonable courage; honesty; integrity; dependability; personal bias or lack of bias; attitudes toward sexuality; prior drug use; and motivation for choosing law enforcement as a career are all assessed Roufa notes that the personality assessment tools used by most agencies have been validated as accurate predictors of behavior over years of study. Police departments and psychologists alike are fairly confident that psychological screening does indeed work because of the vast amount of data available to back up the validity of these tests.[3]

Other "sounds good" recommendations include cultural diversity training and increased recruitment of minorities. In my experience, an eight- or sixteen-hour cultural diversity training program does not change the hearts and minds of those few who engage in police brutality. Minorities are just as likely to engage in misconduct as anyone else when they are indoctrinated into a police culture where they are not held accountable for misconduct. It's clear, however, that police departments know what is required to implement change, and some departments are already doing it. For those changes to take root and establish a solid ethical culture, they must be consistently reinforced.

In 2016, the nonprofit advocacy group Campaign Zero launched the Police Use of Force Project, a study of the use of force in the hundred largest cities in the United States. Based on their work, the researchers recommend eight policies to limit the use of excessive force, and they created a website to track the implementation of those policies around the country (8CantWait.org).[4] Here are their eight recommendations:

1. De-escalate situations whenever possible.
2. Use a force continuum for the appropriate escalation of force.
3. Prohibit the choke hold or stranglehold.
4. Issue verbal warnings whenever possible.
5. Ban officers from shooting at moving vehicles.
6. Exhaust all other reasonable means of intervention.
7. Intervene and stop witnessed incidents of excessive force.
8. Report each time force is used or threatened.

In brief, the report concludes that police departments with all of these policies in place had 72 percent fewer killings than a police department with none in place. The study examined only the number of people killed by police. It did not compare those numbers to arrest numbers, even though the chances of killing a civilian increase with the number of arrests. However, the data suggests that these policies may also be associated with reductions in other forms of police violence—such as assaulting suspects or uttering threatening language at citizens—at least in the cities studied.

Putting such policies in place obviously works, but we need to ensure they are followed. Excessive force is taking a toll. No one wants another act of excessive force by police to harm or end another life. The time for change is now, before there is any further erosion to the bonds between police and the communities they have sworn to serve. Without the partnership of a healthy police-citizen relationship, police are less effective in their sworn duties. Crime witnesses are less likely to come forward. Criminal activity rises. Social and physical disorder rises. We all suffer as our communities are increasingly victimized by bad actors.

In Alexandria, Virginia, Part I offenses such as murder, rape, robbery, aggravated assault, burglary, larceny, vehicle theft, and arson were up 18 percent between January 2019 and September 2020.[5] In Columbus, Ohio, violent crimes were up in 2020 compared to 2019, with homicides ahead of 2019 at the same time and aggravated assaults, rape, larceny trending up.[6] For the month of June 2020, New York City reported an increase in gun violence by 130 percent over June 2019.[7]

Police morale is declining sharply in the face of harsh criticism and falling community trust. Officers in New York City are retiring at alarming rates, police union officials say.[8] Without community trust and cooperation, the brightest and most dedicated officers will keep leaving. Without community support, not only is the job of policing infinitely more difficult, but the intrinsic rewards of protecting and serving are declining. The job, to many, is losing its shine.

No one wants another act of excessive force by police to harm or end another life. No one wants crime to rise with too few officers to respond. We need to act now. The approach I offer in these pages doesn't require permission of governmental bureaucracies, which can take years to obtain. It doesn't require extensive studies or planning to institute. I provide in-house solutions, and they are doable immediately. They will dramatically reduce and even end unethical conduct, and, in doing so, restore an environment of trust, confidence, and cooperation between the public and those who have sworn an oath to serve them. Police departments have all the tools to solve problems of corruption and use of excessive force; all they need to do is implement them through ethics-based policing, a culture grounded in accepting responsibility.

As police improve accountability in their operations, they must also build or repair their relationship with citizens. Much of that construction can be accomplished in-house—the police station house, that is. Resentment and ill will can be reduced and even eliminated if steps are taken to reduce police use of excessive force or police brutality by developing these seven building blocks of police integrity:

- Prudence
- Trust
- Courage
- Intellectual Honesty
- Justice
- Responsibility
- Self-Effacement of Interests

Remember these seven building blocks—we'll return to them repeatedly throughout this book. I've witnessed the use of excessive force by police firsthand, and I've seen how utilizing these building blocks creates change. In 1982, as a newly assigned lieutenant, I had the opportunity to demonstrate my attitude toward honorable policing immediately. I was out with a group of police officers and sergeants on a drug sweep in a ravaged community. We intended to rid the community of street level trafficking. After we identified a street dealer, a foot chase ensued. The dealer was caught and brought back to the center of operations in handcuffs. Upon his return, a veteran sergeant punched him in the mouth—in my presence.

Knowing how essential ethical conduct is to effective policing, I initiated the most severe disciplinary action possible, and I followed through. Statements were taken from all those who witnessed the aggression. The word quickly spread about my strict adherence to ethical conduct, regardless of the bad actor's title or rank. The sergeant in question received a thirty-day suspension from duty without pay.

When I served as an official, the men and women in my department understood I did not condone the use of excessive force. If any issues arose, they came straight to me. They knew I wasn't afraid to investigate, even without a complaint from the victim. Through my willingness to tackle unpleasant situations head-on, officers refused to cover up the bad behavior of other officers due to a misplaced sense of loyalty or fear of repercussions. The blue wall of silence failed. That wall only protects those who should not be in the profession to begin with.

I applaud the officers who came to me with reports of unethical conduct. They had courage. As an insider, I understood they risked retaliation from the bad actors, so it was important for me to follow through, to be consistent in my response to unethical conduct, to weed it out. With dedication and consistency, the use of excessive force under my watch declined by 90 percent. Citizen complaints charging use of excessive force plummeted. I know—I watched those statistics like a hawk.

I wrote this book to stop the use of excessive force. Even though there are fewer offending officers than extensive media reports might imply, those officers should not be on the job. We can only regain the trust, confidence, and cooperation of the communities that police officers are sworn to protect and serve if we reduce the use of excessive force and all other forms of corruption.

The premise of this text is straightforward: the police force can be transformed by ensuring that an ethical police culture is created and consistently maintained by supervisors and mid-level managers. The approach I propose can be acted upon quickly. Successful implementation by the Los Angeles Police Department and others proves its potential to impact failing police agencies, with those in the worst shape showing the greatest improvement.[9]

While there may be other effective remedies to the problem, such as policy or structural changes, legislation, and so on, they can be expensive. None will work as quickly, effectively, or efficiently as the method I am proposing. When supervisors and mid-level managers take responsibility for holding subordinates accountable for their conduct—both exemplary and unethical—everything changes. The responsibility/accountability continuum can be initiated tomorrow at little or no cost.

This book has two parts. Part 1 explores the history of police corruption, how it emerges, its impact on communities, and what is required for change. Part 2 offers a guide for police departments to consider as they implement and strengthen an ethical culture. To illustrate the profound importance and impact of an ethics-based policing, I draw vignettes from over four decades of personal experience in the profession of policing, from my early years as a uniformed patrolman to my final role as a chief of police.

Policing has been my life's work. This book is my invitation to join the call for higher ethical standards to improve the profession. It is my hope that you will find my words useful, and I encourage you to give serious consideration to the value of ethics-based policing.

PART ONE

Understanding the Problem

ONE

Bad Apples or Bad Barrel?

A few bad apples in the barrel spoil the bunch. But what if the barrel itself is bad?

In the 1990s, Steve Vicchio, a medical ethics professor at Johns Hopkins University, extended the popular rotten apple metaphor to police ethics. The roles of both physicians and police require a great amount of discretion, presenting them with the potential for similar ethical issues. Vicchio recognized that not only the apples but the barrel or environment that holds them can cause ethical problems. In policing at present, the most concerning ethical issue is the use of excessive force.

Considering the *Christopher Commission Report* on the Los Angeles riots following the 1991 Rodney King incident and the 2000 Los Angeles *Rampart Corruption Report* investigating allegations of widespread police corruption, Vicchio may be right. Even though those incidents are dated, they demonstrate how compromises in police integrity can go beyond a few bad apples. That suggests the problem, at least in some cases, is the barrel.

A tidal wave of investigations into police corruption is now underway. Some investigations are internal or in-house. Others are conducted by media outlets like *Newsweek*[1] and *USA Today*[2] or on local and national television stations. The Department of Justice, local and state legislators, and independent organizations like the American Civil

3

Liberties Union (ACLU) and Campaign Zero (campaignzero.org) are investigating too. In addition, law firms are actively seeking those with complaints for possible civil litigation.[4]

A quote from the Los Angles *Rampart Corruption Report* draws from my study about work culture and a tendency to lean toward mediocrity rather than excellence:

> As you read this report from the Board of Inquiry, keep Captain Swope's observations in mind for we found, and you will see that mediocrity was alive and well in Rampart up until about 1998. We are sad to report that we also found mediocrity threatening to engulf many of our other workplace environments as well. This is not to say or imply in any way that corruption is occurring throughout the Department, for we do not believe that is the case. However, there are strong indicators that mediocrity is flourishing in many other workplaces and the mindset of too many managers and supervisors is allowing it to occur. Rather that challenging our people to do their best, too many of our leaders are allowing mediocre performance and, in some cases, even making excuses for it.[4]

Accepting mediocre behavior, or failing to hold officers accountable, poisons the barrel. As the corruption report stated, mediocrity threatened to engulf not just the Rampart Division but also other units in the LAPD.

A few unqualified individuals will always find their way into police agencies no matter how rigorous the selection procedures. And make no mistake; selection procedures are rigorous. Initial screening typically includes various questionnaires, oral interviews, physical exams, psychiatric exams, extensive background investigations, and written exams that test math and language proficiency. The last department I worked in yielded only one officer for every twenty-five applications. That's just four percent of those who applied.

Generally, the few undesirable individuals who slip through the selection process are effectively dealt with. They are too few in number to contaminate a police organization. That leads back to culture as the source of problems in some police departments or units. A permissive unethical environment—the unattended bad barrel—can perpetuate root-shaking scandals. Prevailing police culture controls the level of ethical behavior.

Solidarity and shared experiences create strong bonds among officers. Those bonds can build the blue wall of silence or protectionism among ranks. Over time, unchecked solidarity can instill the mantra that police can do no wrong, inviting weaker members to cross the lines of ethical policing, subsequently ensnaring them in a cycle of violence and other unscrupulous behaviors. The concept of "street justice" takes place in departments or units without an ethical police culture. Officers assume they have license to punish offenders outside of the legal system using excessive force. If they suffer no consequence for their actions, the behavior continues.

But here's the good news: a strong ethical culture is just as influential and impactful as a police culture with no moral compass. If department and unit cultures are committed to ethics-based policing, the blue wall of silence cannot exist. Few ethical lapses will occur, and any officers who cross the line will be shunned and reported. A shunned officer is considered untrustworthy and generally unpopular. No one else wants to work with them. That's a miserable prospect for individuals who are so closely connected to their peers on and off duty.

When corporals, sergeants and mid-level managers fail in their responsibility to instill, support, and demand the highest ethical performance from officers in all their duties—when they fail to demand accountability—they relinquish their reins of control. Without ethical guideposts, the culture takes on a life of its own. Sometimes that life is corrupt, brutal, callous, and cruel. Recent events involving the police have demonstrated that an unethical police culture is alive and well in some departments or units.

By contrast, ethics-based policing thrives in a culture where consistent supervision provides clearly conveyed expectations, rewards and recognition for ethical performance and consequences for failures. The culture is one of integrity and ethical service to the public.

Everyone benefits from this culture. Because the police department is trusted, the public is better served. Residents and businesses form productive and responsive bonds. Individual officers perform their duties with dedication, empathy, and commitment because their efforts are respected by those they swore to protect and serve. They end their tour of duty with a sense of accomplishment. They're proud of the professional and disciplined career they have chosen and proud to be in the service of others, many of whom have no one else to turn to for help.

Police officers do not enter the profession to engage in the use of excessive force. They do not view the profession as an opportunity to beat people or violate individual constitutional rights. Unethical, violent behavior is nurtured in the barrel—the culture—of a few police organizations rather than in the character flaws of individuals.

Rotten Barrel History

One quick internet search reveals a plethora of reports on police corruption, past and present. Perhaps one of the most publicized examples of the rotten barrel concept is depicted in the movie *Serpico*, based on the true story of whistleblower Frank Serpico. A patrolman and later a detective in the New York City Police Department, Serpico brought to light the corruption present in the department during the late 1960s and early 1970s. His actions prompted Mayor John Lindsay's appointment of the Knapp Commission to investigate the police department. The Commission found widespread corruption in the NYPD. Unethical behavior was so rampant, it had become an accepted practice. As new officers came on board, they were immersed in the corrupt culture, expected to work within it, and it flourished.

The bad barrel is not a new phenomenon; it is as old as policing itself. Problems with police extortion, use of excessive force, and other shady activities are documented as early as 1844, when the New York

State legislature created its police force as the first municipal police department in the country. The 1890s had the Lexow Commission probe police corruption.[5] In other large US cities, powerful, crooked political machines developed in the latter half of the nineteenth century and effectively thwarted efforts to foster police integrity.

The 1910s saw further investigation into the highly questionable behavior of the NYPD through the Curran Committee,[6] and the Becker/ Rosenthal scandals.[7] In 1931, the Wickersham Commission report documented corruption and brutality in the criminal justice system throughout the United States.[8] From 1930 to 1932, the Seabury Hearings investigated police corruption in New York City as did the Harry Gross Investigation in the 1950s.[9]

Following the 1960s publication of Frank Serpico's story in the *New York Times*, the Knapp Commission hearings disclosed that plain clothes "pads"—money paid to procure protection from arrest—existed throughout the department. To some degree, corruption existed in almost all police units. Bribes and kickbacks were an accepted component of all police operations, among uniform and plain clothes officers alike. Uniformed patrol officers received bribes for special treatment in traffic enforcement among other activities. Plain clothes officers milked those in organized criminal operations. This behavior was so routine that it had become expected. Knowledge about or participation in corruption was characteristic of NYPD culture and it reached from the bottom to the top of the organization. In 1974, the Philadelphia police were accused of engaging in criminal practices at all levels of the police force.[10]

In the 1980s, seventy-five Miami police officers were arrested for serious acts of police corruption. The "Miami River Cops," as some came to be known, were charged with high-level drug dealing and murder.[11] Then there were the shocking abuses of the New Orleans Police Department, where at least fifty police officers were arrested for felonies including homicide, rape and robbery from 1993 to 1996.[12] The *Mollen Commission Report* of 1993 found large scale corruption in the NYPD involving extortion, brutality and theft.[13]

The Christopher Commission, investigating the LAPD after the

Rodney King beating, found that "there is a significant number of officers in LAPD who repetitively use excessive force against the public and persistently ignore the written guidelines of the department regarding force" and that "the failure to control these officers is a management issue that is at the heart of the problem."[14]

The use of excessive force was deemed acceptable. Knowledge of, participation in, or failure to provide vigorous and coordinated oversight ran throughout the organization. Late in 1997 and early 1998, three incidents identified LAPD officers as suspects in serious criminal conduct. This conduct included robbery, false imprisonment, beating a handcuffed arrestee, and theft of drugs from the department's property division. The commission discovered that serious misconduct was pervasive and rampant in the Rampart Division. (More on this later.)

Although fewer studies are conducted in smaller centers, local news reports indicate they are not immune from unethical conduct. Vallejo, California, a city of about 120,000 with a police department of one hundred or so officers, has been plagued by police shootings, costly civil rights lawsuits, and incidents costing more than seven million dollars since 2011. Springfield, Oregon, with a population of just over 63,000, found itself on the wrong end of a federal civil rights lawsuit as a result of police conduct. Allegedly, a protester was violently pulled out of a crowd, knelt on, and punched twice by an officer while under control of other officers, on July 29, 2020. The protester was later arrested.[15]

In 2019, it cost the 176,000 citizens of Oceanside $100,000 in an unreasonable force judgment. The following year, Ontario, California, with a population of 181,000, was charged with a $200,000 excessive force finding.[16]

Finding a Cure

Historically, it's clear that police misconduct is like a persistent virus that lies dormant below the surface. It's discovered, treated, assumed cured, and then forgotten. But over time, the disease of corruption emerges once more. There is really only one cure: persistent, vigorous oversight from first-line supervisors and mid-level managers in a police department where leadership enforces ethics-based policing.

Effective first-line supervisors and mid-level managers are absolutely critical. Say a department institutes a system to track all uses of force. The effort would identify those who engage in the use of force and tag them as potential problems for closer supervision. Issue resolved? Perhaps. But if first-line supervisors and mid-level managers view the tracking system as little more than extra paperwork, if they aren't vigorous in enforcing the new policy with repercussions for offending officers, its intended goal fails.

If the police culture accepts any unethical conduct, new policies and procedures may treat the symptoms without providing a cure. A police department may expand their diversity recruiting and hiring programs, but if those new officers find themselves in a culture where an unethical culture is present, diversity will provide no cure. Additional training, whether it be sensitivity training or studying the Constitution or the social contract theory will not cure the problem in an unethical police culture.

It is essential for the chief executive of any police department to possess and exhibit integrity, but their sterling conduct is not enough. Sergeants, lieutenants, and captains are the last hands in the chain of command to touch the mail. Ultimately, they are responsible for maintaining a sound barrel. Police department rules, regulations, policies, procedures, general orders, and manuals are worthless unless they—the first-line supervisor and mid-level managers—accept the responsibility of holding subordinates accountable for both ethical and unethical behavior. Because they oversee police service and run day-to-day operations, supervisors and mid-level managers have a profound influence on the conduct and behavior of their subordinates. They reinforce or ignore the directions set by the chief of police and thus have the greatest influence over the organizational culture, good or bad.

Police officers are closely attuned to what their peers are doing or not doing. Most officers know who slacks off on the job, who sleeps on duty, and who is quick with violence or engages in the use of excessive force. In a department where ethics-based policing is valued and prevails, officers, supervisors and mid-level managers understand how much influence they have on one another. They work together to maintain integrity. Members of the department are expected to report acts of unethical conduct for investigation, and they are supported in their efforts.

In problem agencies or units, however, unethical conduct is tolerated. Peers and supervisors turn a blind eye or sweep abhorrent behavior under the rug. Sometimes incidents are covered up or ignored, or out of fear or ignorance, are not acted upon. In these situations, the ethical police remain silent. They understand they won't be supported in their claims, and they cannot buck the culture on their own. They cannot risk alienating the men and women they work with and rely upon to have their backs. Unfortunately, over time, unchallenged unethical conduct becomes tolerated and viewed as "the norm," just as the Knapp Commission discovered. Acts of excessive force and unchallenged use of profanity and brutality eventually seem common and unobjectionable.

Building a Sound Barrel

An unsound barrel or environment can be preempted. Once tainted, it can be repaired. If first-line supervisors and mid-level managers hold their subordinates accountable for serving with integrity, the barrel will be solid, the culture ethical.

The good news is that most police officers want to be part of a highly regarded police department free of integrity issues. It's only when some officers engage in use of excessive force without repercussion, without being called to task, that things begin to fall apart. The police cultural barrel weakens, and ethics begin to leak between the cracks. For the growth and maintenance of a healthy culture, sergeants, lieutenants, and captains must respond effectively to any and all use of excessive force by their officers. Their subordinates are watching.

Police officers, investigators, and detectives know when a sergeant or lieutenant accepts or tolerates questionable behavior. They know because they witness their supervisor's response or lack of response to such behavior. An injured arrestee is asked no questions about the source of his or her injuries. A reported unethical act is ignored. When the established culture or habit is to ignore clear misconduct or brush it aside, police officials take no action. Perhaps they don't care, or they want to be popular. Maybe it seems like too much work, they don't know how, or they rationalize that it is not their responsibility.

At what point does questionable conduct become unacceptable? How and where does the line blur? If an unanswered radio call is ignored by mid-level managers, will it become acceptable for officers to routinely select which calls for service they chose to respond to? If punching a passive resister is considered acceptable, will striking a handcuffed prisoner be dealt with or ignored? Superiors who do not take action against the misconduct of one subordinate impact other officers under their charge. They wonder at which point they should report bad behavior. Police executives and department leaders create the barrel framework, but first-line supervisors and mid-level managers form the staves that hold a solid culture of ethics-based policing together. Leadership from the top is important, but supervision and management are critical.

Most sworn officers know what is right and what is wrong. They understand the policies, procedures, and orders of their departments. Most officers do not condone the use of excessive force. The question is, at what point does unethical conduct become unacceptable to the supervisor? It is essential for supervisor and mid-level managers to clearly convey that any use of excessive force is unacceptable, and action will be taken against those who engage in it.

In the absence of a clear and unambiguous message that bad behavior will not be tolerated, some officers may decide that it is safer to remain silent. They cannot and will not risk alienation from their peers, their friends. The people whom they count on to have their backs. If there is any chance the supervisor will not respond appropriately to reports of unethical behavior, officers will feel safer sticking to the code of silence—the blue wall of silence—and defer total responsibility for dealing with unethical behavior to their supervisors. If asked about an act of misconduct, they will deny knowledge of it.

This learned behavior of denial begins when rookies leave the police academy. They are quickly immersed into police culture, guided by senior patrol officers whose behavior they emulate. They observe the rules and attitudes of their superiors, they adopt the values of department culture, and they conform. In an unhealthy ethical culture, the moral compass is dysfunctional. Loyalties lie with their brothers and sisters in service. When ethics-based policing is firmly in place, dedication and commitment lies with values such as upholding the law, agency rules, the police profession itself, and the community being served.

Supervisors are not and cannot be present on every call for service, so officers witnessing unethical misconduct such as the use of excessive force must be willing to come forward. They must be confident that their supervisor will take action. If the supervisor turns a blind eye, officers will also turn a blind eye. They may participate in the misconduct, leave the unit, or even leave the profession.

There is one other option—the "Serpico" option: buck the unethical system/culture.

An officer can rationalize that maintaining an ethical culture is not part of their job; it falls solely on the supervisor. That is what the supervisor gets paid for. This environment, created by the supervisor who fails to clearly convey the proper message, adds brick and mortar to the blue wall of silence. It grows not because the officer lacks integrity, but because the supervision system creates it. I cannot repeat this point enough: If an officer believes nothing will be done with their report of misconduct, it will not be reported. If an officer is confused or in doubt as to the actions his official will take, the misconduct will not be reported.

Imagine, if you will, the message delivered if a superior sees an officer punch a handcuffed prisoner and says nothing. Witnessing officers get the message that abusive behavior is tolerated. If such an event is reported to a superior and ignored, a similar message is sent. Law enforcement agencies that have remained relatively free from the use of excess force have supervisors and managers who know how to respond to unethical conduct, particularly the use of excessive force and brutal-

ity. Their responses create clear guideposts for subsequent moral judgments amongst all officers.

I know the effectiveness of prompt, appropriate responses firsthand.
In the units—the commands—I ran, the expectation for ethical performance of duty was clearly conveyed to all. Officers and police supervisors
set a high bar. Because we were on the same team, we communicated,
cooperated, collaborated, and trusted one another. I observed no hesitation in reporting and investigating acts of misconduct.

Behavior such as officers caught sleeping on high-risk security assignments, acts of sexual harassment and in particular, the use of excessive
force, were promptly reported by witnessing officers. They were reported
because their peers wanted to be part of a disciplined, ethical unit that
did not tolerate wrongdoing. They had confidence in their supervisors,
and they were clear on my directions. They were dedicated to a healthy,
effective police force that protected and served their communities, not
to the protection of those who worked against it.

Even in this seemingly utopian environment there were those who
tested the system. Some failed. On one occasion, a supervisor received
a report that two officers had called out sick and went to New England
to ski. They met up with a third officer who was there on a granted annual leave. The two officers in question had previously requested annual
leave but were denied because of manpower shortages, so their sudden
illnesses seemed suspicious. Calling out sick may have sent them on
their ski trip, but it created forced overtime for the officers who had to
cover for them, an obvious injustice.

The supervisor, a sergeant, questioned the "sick" officers to verify
their condition. They confirmed they were home sick. I directed the
sergeant to ask the third officer—the one who had legitimately taken
leave—if he was with the other two officers in New England skiing.
The third officer refused to answer. The sergeant bumped questioning
to the lieutenant, who again ordered the third officer to respond. He
again refused. Initially I had the impression he was a standup man. So
much for my impressions. I had him brought to me with a direct order to tell me whether he was with the two "sick officers," and that a

refusal to answer would result in disciplinary action. He refused. I immediately removed him from his specialized position and filled it with another officer.

I also initiated adverse action. Disciplinary measures were necessary. How could I or others have confidence in someone who felt they could pick and choose what direct orders they wanted to follow? At the sound of gunshots, would he run toward danger as ordered, or would he choose to run away, failing to protect those he had sworn to serve?

The officer pled his case to a higher authority in an administrative position who quelled the adverse action but was unable to reverse his demotion. When word got out about his penalty, the two officers who had falsely called out sick confessed to me. They were disciplined. Eventually, they recovered and became "top cops"—ethical men of high performance. The third officer, the one who refused a direct order never really got it despite his demotion. He was disciplined several times after that for false statements to a superior officer and became labeled a "Brady Cop" in an official account of his repeated misbehavior.[17]

I encourage law enforcement officials to persevere. There are some police who may never "get it," but as long as they are held accountable for their actions, there is success. Success? Yes, because all those who engage in the ethical performance of their duty see the results of misconduct and unethical conduct, creating guideposts.

There is zero upside for such conduct in an ethical culture. In a healthy work culture, everyone takes responsibility for ethical performance of duty. Everyone understands this responsibility. The system has created an environment where officers will stand up, act responsibly, and report acts of misconduct.

An officer's behavior is influenced more directly by the actions or lack of actions in response to ethical shortcomings of their immediate superiors than by the stated directives or written ethical code of an organization. Regardless of formal ethical codes and policies to prevent the use of excessive force, police are influenced by the standards of behavior they observe in their immediate superiors. They see firsthand how the sergeant or other superior handles a breach in the department's policy on the use of force. That response is critical in maintaining an ethically healthy culture.

Designed for Honesty

According to Aristotle, "Governments and other social institutions should be set up so that is both possible and sensible for people to be honest, loyal, compassionate, and fair."[18] Work environments should not require acts of moral courage to perpetuate ethically responsible behavior. If the culture fosters ethical issues for those who are tasked with controlling crime and meeting community needs, why would officers come forward to report wrongdoing? Doing the right thing is more difficult than it should be, and at times, requires considerable courage.

Police agencies must not allow such a culture to flourish. Everyone within the organization should know that undesirable behavior, such as use of excessive force and brutality, will be challenged, while virtues of prudence, justice, courage, intellectual honesty, responsibility, self-effacement of interests and trustworthiness will be rewarded. Those virtues should be considered standard operating procedure.

Police agencies can build a culture of integrity and high ethical standards by holding those in positions of authority responsible for their subordinates and holding subordinates accountable for their own behaviors. When superiors commit to this pattern of action and consequence, a clear message is conveyed: use of excessive force, brutality, and lack of commitment to the highest standards is unacceptable. That preempts any opportunity for a culture of corruption, criminal behavior and brutality to take hold. When bad behavior can't take hold, the men and women in blue are empowered to perform their jobs with a high level of consistency and integrity.

Clear communication is essential. From an ethics and integrity standpoint, failure to convey and enforce expectations leads to disastrous results. First-line supervisors and mid-level managers must convey the expectation that excessive force will not be tolerated and then reinforce it with quick and vigorous investigations into complaints, dealing appropriately with offenders. A decrease in unethical behavior will follow. If expectations clearly illustrate there is no tolerance for incidents of brutality, violence will decrease. If expectations clearly show that it is unacceptable for members of the police department to accept gratuities and that violators will be dealt with, a decrease in graft and bribes will follow.

Across police agencies, countless policies, procedures, orders, manuals, regulations, and directives of various names, titles, and classifications prohibit unethical conduct. This vast array of guiding material is useless if officers aren't convinced that regulations will be followed. If the message sent makes it clear that following all policies and procedures is vitally important for success, codes of conduct won't be broken. The agency's foundation and public trust will remain intact.

The formal code of ethics or organizational value system can be quite different from the actual culture in which police perform their duty. If the culture is not moderated, violations occur. The use of force, profanity, discriminatory treatment, and differential enforcement of laws for the disenfranchised take root. Alternatively, police supervisors and managers can provide direction in bringing the operational culture of a police department in line with the formal organizational code of ethics. They can do this by constant and consistent actions that convey and reinforce the expectation.

Obviously, a one-time exposure is not enough. Expectations must be conveyed frequently enough to create change. How much time that will take and how often those expectations need repeating will vary according to the level of change required, the seriousness of the problem being addressed, and the intensity of resistance encountered. With serious matters like widespread brutality or use of excessive force, the expectation may have to be communicated before every tour of duty.

Expectations cannot be presented once and then forgotten. If a blind eye is turned, if unethical behavior is tolerated, it will continue. If the barrel is full of holes, it will leak. Continual communication and reinforcement of these expectations are among the primary responsibilities and obligations of sergeants, lieutenants and captains at the helm. Police use of excessive force cannot exist for long without implicit or implied acceptance by supervisors. An agency can double its internal affairs unit, triple the number of integrity checks, and continue to patch the barrel, but those are temporary fixes. The barrel is still rotten.

A more comprehensive approach—a wellness program, so to speak—builds a police culture of accountability from the inside out. Police departments have the capability and responsibility to replace broken staves, to ensure the barrel is sound. They do this by revitalizing and reinforcing their core values in the minds and hearts of all personnel so that each and every police officer understands their responsibility to uphold the standards of their department and ethics-based policing.

Equally important is the need to train first-line supervisors and mid-level managers. When they understand what is required of them and their critical role in police department health, they can create and maintain a department void of brutality, excessive force, and other ethical issues. They are the guardians of a healthy police culture.

TWO

The Ethical Gatekeeper

The following headline appeared several years ago in a major metropolitan area newspaper:

County Police Sued in Dog Bite Incident

In summary, the story stated that a police officer released his dog on two vagrants. Testimony in the resulting civil case revealed that the police officer handling the dog even asked his sergeant, who was present, if it was okay to release the dog.

I found myself dumbstruck. I was also humiliated and embarrassed by the event, not only for myself but also for the police profession. Two questions immediately came to mind. The first: Why would an officer even ask such a question of a sergeant? The second: Why would such an action ever take place? The answer: The department's ethical culture accepted such conduct.

In another part of the country, a police board of inquiry reported that an officer pleading guilty to criminal charges had cooperated with investigators in exchange for a reduced sentence. As a result of the information he provided, investigators discovered that there was much deeper corruption than originally suspected. Once again, I had a question: Where were the first-line supervisors when all that corruption took root?

The answers to the questions noted above are important. Of greater concern is how or why the ethical gatekeepers for the respective police departments failed.

Police agencies have a rank structure and a chain of command much like the military. In an effective chain of command, those in positions of authority—supervisors and mid-level managers—are responsible for the actions of those who are charged with providing service. On the police force, corporals, sergeants, and lieutenants are in the best position to observe subordinate behavior, putting them in the best position to be ethical gatekeepers. They must be charged with the responsibility of defining the ethical culture according to department regulations.

Through daily observation, the ethical gatekeeper can note mistakes, identify weaknesses, and address the shortcomings of their charges. By working side by side with police officers each day to ensure that the integrity standards of their department are upheld—and by holding police officers accountable for their behavior—they can play a major role in preventing ethical failures.

When there is an absence of accountability, little direction, or a lack of discipline, problems arise. At minimum, these problems reflect poorly on a police agency. At worst, they can explode into the kind of nationwide, root-shaking scandals we are observing at the present time. Issues appear, such as brutality and the use of excessive force, irresponsibility, laziness, racism, deviance, abuse of authority, and, ultimately, performance. In the most egregious offence, outcomes include the death of an individual in police custody.

Keys to Ethical Gatekeeping

The ethical gatekeeper holds three keys that are essential to police agency culture: integrity, ethics, and responsibility. These keys are not intended to hang on a ring and be carried around on someone's belt. They must be used and communicated constantly and consistently.

The key of integrity represents the adherence to professional standards. Police departments are guided by written orders, procedures, manuals, policies and regulations, and laws creating a path of professional standards that must be followed.

The key of ethics refers to rules of conduct governing a particular class of human actions. Obviously, in this case, the class of human actions are those of the police officer. Everything an officer should and should not do cannot possibly be included in a department's guidelines, but it is reasonable to assume officers are expected to behave ethically in every situation.

The key of responsibility represents the primary duty of corporals, sergeants, and lieutenants to see that all their behaviors and those of their subordinates are guided by integrity and ethics. As the ethical gatekeepers of the department, they are the subject matter experts on all policies and procedures, and they hold officers accountable for (1) doing what they are supposed to do; and (2) not doing what they are not supposed to do. It's an awesome responsibility.

Police Supervisor Responsibility Scale

The Police Supervisor Responsibility Scale offers three primary supervisor attitudes, each with certain tendencies for demanding accountability from their subordinates. These approaches to accountability establish a culture that permits ethical failures or prevents them:

1. Laissez-Faire
2. Popularity Driven
3. Value Based

Laissez-Faire

The laissez-faire police supervisor holds no subordinate accountable for ethical breaches. They take the hands-off approach. These supervisors rely on avoidance for a variety of reasons. They may be intimidated by subordinates, afraid to make decisions, lazy because of the effort required to hold subordinates accountable, or too timid to face controversy or confrontation. Perhaps they have a poor knowledge of departmental orders and directives or are so inexperienced that they are unsure what needs to be done. They may be untrained in the tenants of supervision, or they may not want to leave their comfort zone.

The laissez-faire police supervisor rationalizes irresponsible behavior. It is no big deal. The perpetrator deserved what they got. Who cares? No one will find out. Or: It is not important. These supervisors fail to see the damaging impact of their failure to investigate complaints. They don't understand the toll of using demeaning language on the job or exerting excessive coercive force or even brutality in the execution of duty. However, the reality is that the public and most police officers do see all of these behaviors as a big deal, so it is particularly important to hold those who engage in misconduct accountable for it.

Laissez-faire supervisors provide little to no supervision, leadership, direction, guidance, or oversight. They do the minimum necessary to survive and get by. They also minimize their own sense of responsibility by deferring most decisions to others.

From time to time in my decades of policing, I encountered a few laissez-faire supervisors. I was embarrassed that they wore the uniform. They did little and their squads suffered for it. Subordinates were left to fend for themselves. With no direction or guidance, some of them were eventually caught up in serious ethical breaches resulting in suspensions or termination. Zero responsibility on the part of the supervisors meant zero accountability from their subordinates.

On the rare occasion laissez-faire supervisors found their way under my command, I brought heat and the hammer. Their next-level superiors worked with them, counseled them, pleaded, cajoled, and threatened. For all intents and purposes, the superiors took over their squad. They were held responsible for their duty or, more appropriately, for a lack of it. Usually, they transferred out or retired. Of course, a transfer generated a notification with words of warning to their new commander.

Popularity Driven

The popularity-driven supervisor is primarily concerned with being everyone's friend. They handle subordinates and situations with kid gloves.

Some see themselves as police force protectors with the mindset of "us" (the police) verses "them" (the public). They are non-confrontational and hold subordinates accountable only when forced to or when doing so supports self-interest. Like laissez-faire police officials, they are prone to rationalization, voicing or internally justifying their action or inaction by saying, "Everybody does it" or "I did it for the officers."

They believe that they are protecting their subordinates. They are not. Their failure to take appropriate action is purely for their own benefit. They want to be seen as the "good guy" in the eyes of those under their charge.

The popularity-driven supervisor sets an unclear or ambiguous ethical tone. Sometimes officers are held accountable, but only when the superior is forced to take action. Popularity-driven supervisors accept ethical failure, shortcomings, and complacency. They can be manipulated. They make excuses for officers' failures as well as for their own. They establish a police culture that invites mediocrity and ethical failures, encouraging the blue wall of silence.

Officers with high ethical values who witness the use of excessive force or brutality will never expose what they have seen to a popularity-driven supervisor because they have no confidence the supervisor will take action. Without confidence, they will not come forward—not because they don't want to or because they accept the misconduct they have seen, but because of the supervisor's attitude. Popularity-driven supervisors permit unethical practices because they do not challenge them. Subordinates become frustrated and discouraged by the lack of discipline, and eventually, unethical behavior spreads to the whole squad, platoon, sector, or department.

Despite their attempts to win approval from their subordinates, I found that first-line supervisors who fell into this misguided role were really not that popular at all. Yes, a few of their favored subordinates found them attractive, but most subordinates viewed them as weak, ineffective, patronizing, and inconsistent. These are less than useful attributes, and they certainly won't permit a supervisor to build an ethical culture.

Value Based

The value-based supervisor holds officers accountable for their conduct. They understand their duty requires maintaining integrity as standard operating procedure and they create a culture that supports it. They operate by rationale. They communicate by word, action, and deed that officers are expected to perform their duties under the guidelines and directives of the department and the law. They call officers to do the right thing. The value-based police supervisor takes responsibility, does not defer or waffle with decision-making. Clear on their duty, these supervisors set a tone of accountability.

It is clear that value-based superiors are the most effective ethical gatekeepers. Because they are clear about what they expect of subordinates, their subordinates trust them. They exemplify and communicate responsible behavior, and they maintain a consistent leadership style. The men and women under their charge can predict how the value-based supervisor will act or react. The officers know they can go to these supervisors whenever they encounter the use of excessive force or any form of unethical behavior among their peers.

Value-based supervisors are the most effective leaders for any police agency. While laissez-fair and popularity-driven supervisors are quick to say they look out for their subordinates, the value-based supervisor is the one who offers the best protection because chances of ethical lapses are reduced. Officers are less likely to engage in brutality and excessive force because they know they will be held accountable. With lower incidents of ethical lapses, the relationship between police departments and citizens is improved.

I was fortunate in my forty-three years of service to work with many value-based supervisors. Their squads performed high operationally, and ethical issues seldom appeared. Esprit de corps was ever present. Each and every officer had trust and confidence in their value-based supervisor. As a result, protecting and serving the public was paramount. Letters of appreciation serve witness to their dedication to duty. A woman whose home was broken into wrote, "As a former newspaper reporter,

I have met many police officers who were handling cases. These three were the finest I have ever encountered. Since I was home at the time the break and enter occurred, I was terrified. They managed to keep me calm while they went about their responsibilities as police officers."

One letter came from the supervisor of a group home for troubled teenage girls who occasionally had need for police assistance. She noted that officers were sometimes reluctant to file reports on resident behavior, and that meant the girls didn't take the police seriously. She was, however, impressed by one officer's response to twins caught smoking marijuana. The officer was "very understanding of the situation and immediately made the girls [who were being flippant] cognizant of his authority and how he would exercise it. He also talked with all of the girls as a group and I believe their respect for the law was increased by the manner in which he performed his job."

After a burglary, one grateful citizen reported that "I was treated to behavior so courteous and professional that I immediately began to calm down. Then they attacked the investigation with a vengeance I've seen in television police shows but didn't believe existed in real policemen working on a small burglary. Three hours later, they called me at work to let me know they had apprehended three suspects and recovered most of the burgled items."

Ethics-based policing is the kind of policing we all want.

Negative Accountability Continuum

Whether holding an officer accountable for a minor infraction such as coming to inspection in a uniform that looks like it was slept in or a more serious violation like striking a handcuffed suspect, the whole point is to *do* something. It requires ethical gatekeepers to choose value-based accountability. The laissez-faire supervisor holds no one accountable or responsible. The popularity-driven supervisor only holds subordinates accountable when they have no other choice. The value-based supervisor always holds subordinates accountable. Their subordinates know it, so they act accordingly. They behave ethically and report unethical behavior because they simply cannot look the other way. They must take action.

Similar to the use of *force continuum* there is an *accountability continuum*. In the use of force continuum, a police officer responds to a given situation with an appropriate level of force on an escalating scale that ranges from the officers' mere presence to lethal force. The accountability continuum also escalates according to the severity of the situation at hand. In response to negative behavior, the accountability continuum might escalate like this:

- A look of displeasure
- Words of reprimand
- Informal counseling
- A negative note in a performance evaluation
- Documented counseling
- Disciplinary action
- Suspension
- Termination
- Criminal charges

First-line supervisors and mid-level managers may not be in the position to carry through on all of these actions without support from their chain of command. For example, with serious administrative action like suspension, termination, or criminal charges, they may require approval from the agency's chief of police. However, they are certainly in a position to initiate action, and they have a duty to do so. Police supervisors hold legitimate authority to ensure their subordinates behave ethically in the line of duty.

When ranking police officials do not agree with supervisor recommendations, supervisors may feel a lack of support. However, their efforts to respond appropriately to ethical issues are never fruitless. The main point of holding subordinates accountable is to take some form of action. Even if that action does not bring the results the supervisor recommended, the subordinates in question still know they are being called to task. Their peers know they are being called to task. It's no secret. It isn't meant to be a secret. So, even if the recommendation isn't approved, it is unlikely the offending officer or their peers will repeat such conduct.

Officers turn to their supervisors for guidance and direction because they view them as authority figures with more experience in the field, a greater understanding of departmental rules and regulations and the law, and plenty of book knowledge under their belts. Enforcing accountability conveys authority, guidance, and direction clearly.

Accountability should be applied to virtually every aspect of duty, from how offices speak with citizens on a traffic stop to how they manage the use of force. Accountability demands that officers do what they are supposed to do and don't do what they are not supposed to do. If police officers behave with a high level of ethical conduct, they can reasonably expect support from the community they're serving. That support is crucial to the effectiveness of any police agency.

During my career with the Metropolitan Police Department in Washington, DC, I sat on a trial board with two other ranking police officials. It was our responsibility to serve as judges for administrative trials when police officers were charged with offenses of the most serious nature. The city attorney would present evidence against an officer, and another attorney would speak on the officer's behalf. Witnesses were called by both sides. At the conclusion of an inquiry, the three ranking officials at the helm were supposed to come to an agreement. Upon reaching an agreement, a findings and recommendation report would be completed for the chief of police.

In one particular case, an officer was charged with falsifying his application to the department. Before filling out the application, the officer had been charged with a multi-count indictment for welfare fraud, pleading guilty to three misdemeanors. On the application, he denied ever having been arrested, indicted, charged, or the subject of a judicial summons in any jurisdiction. Somehow the background investigator failed to uncover the fact that the applicant had indeed been indicted and plead guilty. The applicant was hired. Somewhere around eighteen months into the job, the incriminating information was discovered, leading to charges and the trial board.

We three judges met for many hours to discuss the case in the attempt to reach a unanimous decision. All of those attempts failed, and we agreed to disagree. I wrote a dissenting opinion to the majorities' findings. In brief, the majority determined that although the officer was not performing at a high level, duties were performed without issue. The department's failure to uncover the misdeeds was the issue, not the officer's faulty application. Therefore, they felt the officer should not be held accountable after the fact.

My dissent centered upon the ethical issues and the criminal conduct of the officer: falsifying welfare documents and then falsifying the application. Those offenses meant the officer would never be permitted to perform full police duties and, consequently, was unable to do his job. Officers with a confirmed record of knowingly lying in an official capacity—such as on an application—are exposed to examination by the defense in criminal trials. Their previous dishonesty discredits any testimony they might offer. Prosecutors are required to notify a defendant and their attorney when any police officer with such a history is involved in a case. In my experience, a prosecutor will dismiss the case rather than put a so-called "Brady Cop" on the stand if that officer is key to a conviction.

The ultimate abettor of a trial board decision is the chief of police. While it is difficult to rule against a unanimous recommendation of three ranking policing officials, a police chief may be inclined to choose another solution if the decision is not unanimous. The fact that I submitted a dissenting opinion gave the chief of police an option. He exercised that option, went with the dissenting opinion, and terminated the officer.

I relay this story for several reasons. My colleagues on the trial board were of the highest caliber. One was senior to me in rank. I found their performance of duty to be ethical, with this exception. Instead of being objective, they were sympathetic to the subordinate in question. In their view, the officer was not at fault; it was the department's failure.

While the department did indeed fail to discover the prior criminal conduct of this police officer before hiring, from my perspective, their lack of discovery did not mitigate the criminal conduct. Most disturbing to me was the response I received to a question I raised during our deliberation: Would an officer's prior conviction for assault or domestic violence be acceptable? They informed me that because they believed it was the department's failure, not the officer's, the nature of the prior conviction was of no consequence.

From time to time, I have seen police officials grasp at straws in an effort to explain or excuse unacceptable conduct. This response is an invitation to even more of the same kind of behavior—mediocre performance, unethical conduct, and scandals—any of which could rock a police agency to its core, staining the police profession in general.

It is essential that decision makers strictly adhere to the seven police core virtues: prudence, trust, courage, intellectual honesty, justice, self-effacement of interests, and responsibility. We'll explore those qualities in some depth in the next chapter, but let's take a look here at how they apply to the situation of the improperly hired police officer.

1. *Prudence* is the skill of good judgment and the use of good ethical sense. In the above case, the offending officer had a criminal record and falsified their application, clearly showing poor judgment and a lack of good ethical sense.
2. *Trust* requires character, ability, strength, and honesty. Decision makers must sometimes reach difficult findings but doing so inspires trust from their subordinates and the public. Two of the decision makers in this case failed to reach the logical conclusion suggested by all the facts.
3. *Courage* is required to make difficult findings, but one must have the moral strength and mental strength to persevere. Two of the decision makers were unable to persevere in a difficult situation long enough to make an honest decision.
4. *Intellectual honesty* means allowing one's decisions to be guided by intellect rather than emotion. It displays rational conduct and

the application of knowledge. When the officer's history was discovered, they knew that officer would be considered a "Brady Cop," complicating any litigation that officer might be involved in. Emotion rather than fact guided the majority decision.

5. *Justice* was not served with the initial decision. Sympathy clouded impartial judgment. As a result, their finding did not display equity, nor a righteous, impartial, fair determination according to the rules of law.

6. *Self-effacement of interests* did not play a role. The other two judges were more interested in protecting the accused than taking the appropriate actions on behalf of the agency and the public.

7. *Responsibility* for choosing between right and wrong begins at the top. A culture of ethical conduct and high performance for the public good cannot be created or maintained without everyone on board, without exerting a significant effort toward these goals. If these high-level police operatives could not make an honest, reliable decision when faced with difficult circumstances, how can they expect their subordinates to?

Positive Accountability Continuum

Accountability and discipline aren't pavement markings on a one-way street. One direction holds members accountable for misconduct and unethical behavior. The other equally essential direction holds them accountable for their successes, good work, and outstanding performance. Reinforcing positive direction is just as influential and important as reprimanding negative direction.

Positive discipline sets guideposts, reinforces good work, raises morale, and builds trust. The three keys held by the ethical gatekeeper—integrity, ethics, and demanding accountability from subordinates—cannot completely unlock doors to public trust without positive discipline. It is true that negative discipline can improve accountability but using it exclusively—without positive discipline—falls short of enlightened leadership. A police supervisor who relies solely on negative discipline is not performing responsibly. If responsibility means discharging one's obligations in the performance of duty, isn't that police superior obliged to recognize and reward those who excel and perform with high ethical values?

A highly ethical culture is built on trust, not fear. Trust grows from constant, consistent, clear conveyance of ethical expectations through both positive and negative discipline. As Xenophon, an ancient Greek General once said, "Men who think that their officer recognizes them are keener to be seen doing something honorable and more desirous of avoiding disgrace."[1]

In response to positive behavior, the accountability continuum might look like this:

- A major award
- Written request for formal commendation sent to the police commander
- Public recognition
- Written commendation by supervisor
- Positive note in performance evaluation
- Praise before peers
- Words of praise
- A nod of approval

Once again, the point is to do something. Do something to reinforce the positive behavior so the message is clearly sent. Recognition is a strong motivator.

The three types of supervisors on the Police Supervisor Accountability Scale will apply positive discipline in different ways. Laisse-faire police supervisors won't recognize, reward, or acknowledge officers for good work. Since they fail in this important mission, they fail to show others what constitutes good, ethical police work. The laisse-faire supervisor is similarly inactive with the rational that the officers who did good work were just doing their job. No big deal; no response necessary.

Oh, but it is a big deal!

By refusing to acknowledge good work, an important opportunity is missed to promote, reinforce, display, and communicate superior ethical police service and its importance. Popularity-driven police supervisors recognize everyone for doing anything—or at least those with whom they believe they are popular. This dilution renders all recognition and rewards useless. Everyone views them as meaningless gestures. Many officers feel patronized.

On the other hand, value-based police supervisors continually recognize noteworthy police work performed with integrity and ethics. Praise from a value-based police supervisor has meaning for the recipient as well as the recipient's peers. Recognition and rewards are earned. They set examples and guideposts for all police officers in the unit.

The level of ethical practices that a corporal, sergeant, and lieutenant instill in the officers for whom they are responsible has a significant impact on those subordinates, their peers, the department, the community, and the police profession. The conduct and behavior of ethical gatekeepers affects the reputation of the officers and the agency, the morale of the officers, the public's satisfaction with the police and thus their operational and administrative effectiveness, and ultimately, the culture and integrity of the police profession in the United States.

The conduct of police officers is tied directly to the first-line supervisors and mid-level managers who influence what officers do and what officers fail to do. In the dynamics of ethical police service, many of the influences impacting police personnel are controlled or influenced by the supervisor. That gives corporals, sergeants, and lieutenants the most ability of anyone to maintain or create an organizational culture of highly ethical conduct.

A lieutenant I worked with nicknamed "the Duke" personified the effective ethical gatekeeper. I encountered the Duke and his platoon of officers when I was transferred to a new command as a newly promoted captain. I frequently heard others say, "The Duke don't dance." I soon discovered what that meant. The Duke expected the best out of his officers. He held them accountable for their actions and performance of duty. Perfect uniform and appearance, clean scout cars, professionalism when dealing with the public, and effectiveness in performance were just some of his tenets.

The Duke knew that appearances sent a message to the public. The way officers talked to the public impacted their level of satisfaction with the police. He would not accept poorly prepared police reports or late reporting for an assignment. Although these may seem like minor issues, in totality they had a large impact. His strict demands sent a clear message and established guideposts. Officers were expected to follow the rules and regulations—all the rules and regulations— including those concerning coercive use of force.

I eventually learned that when he had first taken over his platoon, some officers grumbled. A few transferred out. After several months however, with the development of the cliché, "The Duke don't dance," officers no longer spoke in negative terms. They began to consider themselves fortunate to be under the Duke's command. As the months passed, the Duke's reputation spread. In fact, a list grew of officers waiting to be assigned to his platoon.

The level of accountability and discipline to which this lieutenant held his subordinates resulted in a unit that received the most challenging assignments and the most awards and recognition. It had the highest esprit de corps, the most professional performance, the best appearance, and the highest prestige. His platoon was the "go to" unit when things absolutely had to get done, as directed, on time, effectively, and efficiently.

I saw the platoon's skills at work firsthand on several large mass demonstrations—compliant ones, non-compliant ones, and violent ones. There was no use of excessive force, no use of profanity, no brutality in any of those demonstrations. Yes, at times there were arrests, sometimes mass arrests, but in each situation, all directions and department regulations were followed. Why? Because the Duke set police department culture at a high bar. Ethical conduct was expected and conveyed during every tour of duty.

The Duke was very effective in his primary job: getting the work done with a high level of integrity while maintaining productive relationships with his subordinates. Adherence to professional standards, answering to one's conduct, discharging one's obligations to duty, and following established rules of conduct became the culture and standard operating procedure in virtually everything those under his command did. This ethical gatekeeper also presented an excellent role model for his peers and sergeants. He seemed to have extended the value statement of General Ronald R. Fogleman to his police operations: "We have become convinced of the need to continually articulate the core values of our institution. These ideals are at the heart and soul of our military profession: integrity first, service before self, and excellence in all we do."

The Duke accomplished this by holding his officers accountable.

It is true that a sergeant may not be able to change their police department, but they can change their squad. A lieutenant may not be able to change their department, but they can change their platoon. In the future, some of these sergeants and lieutenants will become captains and majors or even the chief of police, and they have the power to create deep change within a department. In the future, the officers who worked with these ethically grounded sergeants and lieutenant will become sergeants and lieutenants themselves. They will then become role models for others, working to change their squads or platoons.

Holding subordinates accountable reduces mediocre performance, brutality, malfeasance, use of excessive force, and other forms of misconduct. It sets an environment with high morale and high performance that serves the public well. In this kind of environment, idealistic, highly motivated men and women can sustain their idealism and motivation. Ethical gatekeepers—police corporals, sergeants, and lieutenants—hold the keys of integrity, ethical behavior, and accountability. They have the duty, obligation, and responsibility to see that police officers and detectives always do the right thing.

It takes courage, commitment to values, effort, knowledge, and steadfastness to do what is required in creating and maintaining a culture based on ethical values. As the late General of the Armies, John J. Pershing, U. S. Army once said, "A competent leader can get efficient service from poor troops, while on the contrary an incapable leader can demoralize the best troops."

Ethical Lapses at the Top

"Power tends to corrupt; absolute power corrupts absolutely."

Lord Acton's words are worth bearing in mind as we examine ethics within a police department or any other organizational structure. Even the best gatekeepers may have their efforts thwarted if ethical lapses exist at higher levels of governance.

So let's venture into the hypothetical. Say the first-line supervisors of most police departments have accepted responsibility for holding subordinates accountable. They understand the critical nature of their role. They know those who exercise high ethical values consistently in their performance of duty deserve to be recognized and rewarded for their work. They also know that doing so will demonstrate the value of good work and set an example for others in the department. The supervisor conveys those ideas clearly. They are committed to always calling out those who fail to perform ethically.

With the practice of supervisor responsibility and officer accountability firmly in place, let's visit an evening tour of duty. Two police units are dispatched for an assault in progress, and a sergeant advises that he is also on the way. One patrol unit arrives first to find the suspect, a middle-aged male, punching an elderly gentleman. As the marked car approaches, a foot chase ensues. Just as the sergeant arrives, the suspect is apprehended by the pursuing officer. The sergeant witnesses the officer handcuff the subject and subsequently punch him in the head, knocking him to the ground.

After the suspect is taken to the station and charged, the arresting officer completes the paperwork. The sergeant who witnessed the arrest calls the officer into the office and directs him to write a statement concerning his aggression toward the handcuffed prisoner. The sergeant conducts an investigation into the incident and recommends bringing formal administrative charges against the offending officer.

Good so far, right? Let's step back a bit.

As officers pursue their careers, they make close friends. Very close friends. Of those friends, some advance in rank. It just so happens that the officer charged in the incident described above had a very close friend who was a senior police official. The formal disciplinary charges against that officer traveled up the chain of command until they reached the senior command official who was his friend. The command official did not concur with the sergeant's investigation or recommendation for formal action. He suggested that only minor corrective action was necessary and stopped formal disciplinary action. Considering that the officer's aggression was witnessed directly and violated the ethical use of force, it seems obvious that the command official made that decision because of his close friendship with the officer involved.

From bottom to the top, including support from the chief, members of the police force who exhibit low core virtues must be held accountable for their actions. Any potential for protection from senior officials must be neutralized, all consideration granted by high-ranking friends eliminated, and efforts to minimize any form of misconduct reduced. When a higher-ranking police official overlooks misbehavior, it not only compromises their personal integrity but also undermines the efforts and motivation of subordinate supervisors to do the right thing. That has the potential to destroy any further attempts to hold those with low core virtues accountable and responsible.

All supervisors impact their subordinates, regardless of their rank. Unethical intervention on the part of a senior command police official spreads through an agency like wildfire. On the job, someone who is protected in this way is said to have a "rabbi." This kind of protection cannot be kept secret and is demoralizing for everyone else within the agency.

During my career on a major metropolitan police department, a captain was stopped by a patrol officer for driving while intoxicated. The captain apparently did not wish to be arrested, and a fight with the patrol officer ensued. The intoxicated captain lost that round, was taken to the station for processing, then to the central cell block. It was not long before his close friend showed up: an assistant chief of police. The assistant chief of police ordered the captain's release. All charges were nullified, and the captain walked out as if nothing had happened. Following the incident, this captain was appointed two political promotions before he retired.

In another situation, a high-ranking police official gave his administrative lieutenant an unethical hand up. His lieutenant had applied for a promotion to captain and completed the initial stage of the process, a written exam. Typically, only lieutenants who score in the top twenty for that exam are invited to the next stage. When the command official's lieutenant didn't make the top twenty, the command official extended the cutoff point from twenty to thirty, allowing his lieutenant to move forward.

During the next stage, the competing lieutenants met with the oral board. The oral board, composed of captains, knew what had transpired. They understood that repercussions loomed if they didn't allow the lieutenant to move forward. As a result, the favored lieutenant received a score from the oral board far higher than anyone else, vaulting him to the number one spot. He was promoted to captain. Before he retired, he received three political promotions.

Although these examples have nothing to do with the use of excessive force or brutality, they have much to do with a command structure that sometimes fails to conduct duties ethically. The message sent by favoritism and favors is loud and clear: cronyism is alive and well. Accountability for the ethical performance of duty—simply doing the right thing—only applies to their subordinates.

The ethical breaches described eventually generated frustration and disappointment in the first-line supervisors and mid-level managers who were charged with creating a culture of integrity. It made their job much more difficult because their subordinates were well aware of the corrupt conduct of police command officials. While cronyism may or may not have been voiced often, it had a profound effect on everyone, those with high core virtues and those with low core virtues. The unprincipled conduct of ranking officials loomed over those in the rank and file, creating an unnecessary hurdle to building or maintaining a highly ethical culture.

These are not isolated instances. There is a history of high-level law enforcement leaders bending or breaking rules and regulations, often confident they would not face accountability for their conduct. With so much power, some police leaders lose their moral compass. The more power some gain, the less ethical sense they exhibit—especially when there is an absence of ethical oversight. In fact, many are shocked when they are called to task for their ethical shortcomings.

Please note the use of the term "law enforcement" and not "police," who are just one element of law enforcement. This issue is just as present in federal investigative agencies as it is policing.

Police Officers Want Accountability

A vivid portrayal of leadership responsibility and subordinate accountability is demonstrated in the movie *Twelve O'clock High* starring Gregory Peck. Set in Europe during World War II, the story involves a bombing wing flying B-17s that conducted daylight sorties against German targets in occupied Europe. This bombing wing was afflicted with high casualties, low morale, low confidence, high sick calls, an absence of military bearing, a failure to take responsibility, and poor performance, as indicated by continuously missing their mission targets. The military officer at the head of this bombing wing not only accepted these conditions but enabled them by rationalizing these serious deficiencies to himself, his subordinates, and his superiors.

Peck's character replaced the officer in charge and immediately took steps to turn things around. He held subordinates accountable for their actions. In doing so, he eliminated the failures that had plagued the unit under the previous leader.

All of this responsibility and accountability sounds good for the department, but it also raises the question, "How are the officers going to feel about it?"

During an effort to identify issues that needed to be addressed to improve a large East Coast police department, a cohort of fifteen experienced officers participated in a facilitated discussion. These officers unanimously identified discipline as the number one issue needing improvement. Specifically, they expected supervisors to consistently hold officers accountable for their conduct. The officers in this cohort were simply shocked at how much some officers were able to get away with.

Police officers want to be part of a disciplined, responsible, accountable organization rooted in integrity. They want "SLAPs" (stupid lazy-ass police) held to task. They want to be part of an organization that they can be proud of and the public admires. They want their efforts to provide intrinsic rewards, such as satisfaction for a job well done. Police officers want to work in a high-performance ethical and operational culture. Most know right from wrong, as well as what they should do and what they should not do. They seek an ethical culture where what's right is done, what should be done is done, and what should not be done is not done.

THREE

The Police Core Virtue Bell Curve

At present, the reputation of the police profession is at an all-time low. As a result, the profession suffers from fewer intrinsic rewards, a poor relationship with the public, reduced job satisfaction, and decreased morale. This is not impacting just a few isolated neighborhoods. It's affecting communities across the nation, regardless of socio-economic strata, ethnicity, political affiliation, or demographic.

Acts of police brutality and use of excessive force have shaken public trust and confidence to the core. In some areas, hostility is so endemic that all police use of force is considered wrong—even if it's required to save a life. In a recent case, major disturbances erupted when a vehicle pursuit resulted in a crash. The suspect had lost control of their vehicle and succumbed to the injuries sustained. High-profile events such as this one generate a barrage of questions both inside and outside police agencies. How did we get to this point? What can be done about it? How can events like these be prevented in the future?

Seven Core Virtues

A certain key aspect of integrity has long been missing in the policing profession and indeed beyond: supervisors who take the responsibility to hold their subordinates accountable. Without consistently imposing consequences for behavior—good and bad alike—considerable problems result. It leads to laziness, a lack of commitment, and the excessive tolerance that fuels corruption, brutality, and the use of excessive force, specifically in law enforcement at any level and particularly in the current environment.

For ethics-based policing to thrive, police officers must consistently utilize the seven core virtues I pointed out in chapter 2: prudence, trust, courage, intellectual honesty, justice, self-effacement of interests, and responsibility. Let's take a closer look at each one.

Virtue 1: Prudence

Prudence is the skill of good judgment that inspires self-discipline and self-control and expresses caution toward danger and risk. Police are entrusted with immense authority and power. To merit that honor, they are held to a higher standard than the general public. They are expected to exercise restraint in situations where others might respond with fear or aggression. They must remain calm in the face of abuse, only depriving someone of freedom or exercising the use of nonnegotiable, coercive force when prescribed by the law—and then, using only the minimum force necessary. If a handcuffed prisoner spits in an officer's face, for example, prudence demands temper control. Despite how disturbing the incident may be or how offended the officer feels, the officer must exercise enough self-control to implement nonviolent approaches that will prevent a repeat of that behavior.

Police must be vigilant and cautious toward danger, risk, and physical harm to themselves. At the same time, they must also be vigilant about using their authority and power according to the guidelines set forth in regulations, the law, and ethical good sense.

Virtue 2: Public Trust

Public trust is essential to the police. When public trust is in place, individuals and communities are confident the police will protect and serve them. They rely on the character, ability, strength, and honesty of the police, upon whom they have bestowed extensive power and authority.

In the commission of a violent criminal incident with witnesses, they report to the interviewing officer or detective what they saw. They come forward and provide information critical to the identification and apprehension of the perpetrator.

Virtue 3: Courage

Courage calls on officers' mental and moral strength. They must venture into danger and persevere through any fear or difficulty. Courageous police officers have the moral strength to do something about the use of excessive force and brutality. They do not engage in it, thus setting a positive example for their peers. They are committed to reporting any such behavior conducted by their peers, again setting an example. They have the character to respond to difficult and sometimes dangerous activity despite any fear they may have, and they have the ability to control that fear. Courage is far more than the spirit enabling them to face physical danger and pain; it enables them to maintain integrity in whatever situation they find themselves.

Countless times, I heard police radio dispatchers request any available unit to respond to a "man with a gun, armed robbery in progress, reported shots fired, assault in progress," with no fewer than four units responding, "Code One." That means they expedited their response with emergency lights and sirens.

Throughout my police career, subordinates came forward and reported misconduct. At times, I've seen police officers arrest other police officers for criminal offenses. During one midnight tour of duty, I attended the scene of a traffic accident. The vehicle had struck a bridge abutment, and the driver, a police officer, remained behind the wheel with a minor head injury. The police officer called to the scene found the driver was intoxicated. He called an ambulance and placed the officer, who was from his department, under arrest. Another officer rode in the ambulance. Following treatment, the arrested officer was returned to the station for processing.

In another incident, I went to a call for a domestic. When I arrived, I observed a woman I recognized as a police officer in handcuffs. I was informed that she had beaten up her girlfriend, and she was under arrest. This takes courage on the arresting officer's part; they know they are initiating a life-changing action for the arrested officer.

Virtue 4: Intellectual Honesty

Intellectual honesty is developed and chiefly guided by the intellect rather than emotion. It enables rational conduct that calls for reflection and speculation regarding one's actions. It includes the ability to learn, understand, and deal with new and trying situations. Because it requires the application of knowledge to the quality of honesty, it remains free from fraud or deception.

Honest police officers are reputable, respectable, worthy, creditable, and forthright. In addition to being fair and straightforward in their conduct, they adhere to the facts and actively follow the standards of the police profession.

Consider an officer who pulls over a vehicle for exceeding the posted limit by twenty-five miles per hour. The frantic mother behind the wheel makes the excuse that she had to work late and is overdue to pick up her baby from the sitter. Though empathizing with the woman, an officer must keep the public safe, so a ticket is issued in a polite, calm, and respectful manner.

Virtue 5: Justice

Justice involves weighing judgment between conflicting claims with a righteous, impartial, fair determination of rights according to the rules of law and equity.

Say an officer is called to a major chain grocery store. The manager informs him that two children who were playing alone in the store as their mother shopped had knocked over a display of expensive products, breaking several. The manager wants the mother to pay for the damage, and if she refuses, he wants the children taken to juvenile services. The officer learns that the manager didn't see the incident, but the mother freely admits one of her children did cause the damage—*accidentally.* After carefully recording notes about what happened, the officer informs the manager that because the behavior was accidental and not a criminal act of destruction, charges are unwarranted. If the manager is dissatisfied, he can speak with an attorney regarding the incident.

Virtue 6: Self-effacement of Interests

Self-effacement of interests means putting others before oneself. Sometimes, that calls for sacrifice. Consider an on-duty officer who is happy to be called to the station for relief of duty because his son's basketball championship game is about to start and he promised to attend. On the way back to the station, the officer sees a disabled car stopped in the traffic lane of a major artery. Rush hour is approaching, and traffic is already starting to back up. The officer could pass the information on to his relieving officer, but that would delay any response for at least twenty minutes. In that time, the disabled car could be struck by one of hundreds of commuters. If an emergency arose, response vehicle might not get through in a timely fashion.

The officer has a choice. Stopping to assist means missing the first part of the basketball game and delaying a promise. The officer chooses to put personal interests aside and stop behind the broken-down car to help the distraught driver and restore traffic flow.

Virtue 7: Responsibility

Responsibility is the commitment to answer for one's conduct and obligations. It requires the ability to choose between right and wrong and demonstrate integrity in the conduct and performance of duty. In ethics-based policing, supervisors hold their subordinates accountable for unfulfilled trust or violated obligations but also reward them for any duties they fulfill with integrity.

Sometimes, the line between right and wrong behavior may seem gray. After two officers quietly deal with a disorderly patron at an exclusive steak house, the manager insists that they stay and have dinner on him. When they explain they cannot accept gifts for their service, the manager gives them his card and tells them to come in on his dime anytime—on or off duty—and to bring their spouses. Understanding this kind of favor is not permitted, the two officers never take the manager up on his gracious offer.

If deeply engrained, core virtues of prudence, trust, courage, intellectual honesty, justice, self-effacement of interests, and responsibility create external reflections of high standards and traits of ethical behavior. Each of these virtues are at the center of ethical police culture and conduct.

Examining the Bell Curve

With respect to core virtues, the police fall into the same bell curve as society as a whole. Some officers exhibit few of the core virtues. Many officers exhibit some of the core virtues, and some exhibit most or all of the core virtues.

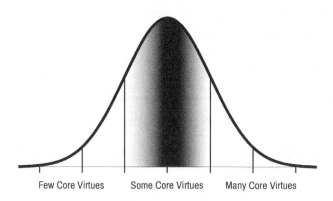

Few Core Virtues   Some Core Virtues   Many Core Virtues

That may sound like an interesting theory, but what does it have to do with ethical conduct in a police organization? Core virtues are displayed on a sliding scale. The level of ethical conduct displayed by any police force depends on the degree of influence exerted by those on the upper and lower sides of the scale in the Police Core Virtue Bell Curve. As we've seen, the immediate supervisors of police officers—corporals, sergeants, and lieutenants—control the nature of that influence.

The chief executive of a police department and all senior managers must possess the seven core virtues and lead by example. They must conduct themselves with a level of integrity visible to all. Expectations for the same behavior from everyone else must be communicated through written regulations, directives, and orders clearly defining ethical conduct. The values and virtues set by a police executive must be communicated from the top down, consistently and continually.

Integrity by example is a start, but it is not enough. If it were, the policing might not be experiencing such disfavor. Responsibility and accountability are key. Supervisors must take the responsibility to hold their subordinates accountable. Without a conscious, deliberate system that holds members accountable for their conduct and any failure to follow departmental policy and procedures, ethical failures will occur. Ethical failures foster a culture where a few police officers will become comfortable engaging in unethical use of force because no one is acting to stop them, and their behavior will grow worse.

Supervisors Create the Culture

All rules, regulations, directives, and written policies and procedures aimed at the issue of integrity are not effective unless they are accepted and applied by the corporals, sergeants, and mid-level managers in a police department. These men and women control day-to-day operations at the ground level. They either interact with subordinates to provide supervision, observation, training, guidance, and accountability, or they do not.

Serious problems arise when they don't take their responsibility seriously. I saw evidence of this on one occasion in early 2006. I was informed that an officer under my charge had been arrested in a nearby county and charged with Drunk in Public and Assault on a Police Officer. Let's call him William. A state-of-the-art video recording of the incident, crystal clear with zooming and scrolling features, shocked me to the core. William had closed down a watering hole in a huge shopping center. As he crossed the parking lot and headed toward home in a drunken stupor, he stumbled and fell. The video zoomed into the scene. Security officers checked on his welfare, but he waved off any help. The video showed William scrambling back to his feet and stumbling again.

Other security officers who were watching the unfolding scene on camera in the control room called the County Police.

Two marked units arrived and approached William, one operated by a female officer, the other by a male officer. William waved them off with no contact, but the male officer grabbed him and threw him to the ground. No exchanges could be heard between them and there were no observable threats, so the aggression appeared unwarranted. William was then handcuffed and thrown into the back of the female's marked car. Moments later, with no reason apparent on the video, the male arresting officer grabbed the handcuffed, drunken William by his feet and dragged him out of the female's marked car, letting his face and head bounce to the ground. He shoved William, who was still handcuffed, into the front seat of his marked car, and belted him in place. Then he jumped into the passenger seat, straddled William, and began hammering him with elbows to the face.

Nothing I had seen on that video warranted the egregious attack on William, yet the officer battered his face until it looked as though he had gone twelve rounds with Mike Tyson.

A week or so later, after I pulled the video and several photographs together, I had coffee with the county police watch commander who had been in charge the night of the incident. Through our discussion, it became clear that his agency culture had no oversight and cared little about ethics. He was unwilling to hold anyone accountable for the unwarranted assault on my officer, even though the attack was recorded in living color. My tolerance for such conduct is ZERO. In the following weeks, I presented the county chief of police—the watch commander's boss—with the video evidence of the shameful event. Later, after he dealt with the watch commander, he extended the profession courtesy of letting me know the outcome. I was satisfied that justice was done.

Bad things happen when there is no accountability. No one is safe, not even other police officers.

Police officers are well aware of what their fellow officers are doing, how they conduct themselves, how they perform their duties, and whether they carry out their obligations. On a misdemeanor theft report, officers know which peers conduct comprehensive preliminary investigations by canvasing the area for witnesses, evidence, and stolen property. They are aware of officers who conduct thorough follow-up investigations. Over the car radio, they hear who makes traffic stops and engages in field interrogations. They can assess who regularly takes long breaks during busy times, and they know those who "hoodle" or park their marked cars and spend long periods talking to other officers or sleeping. They instinctively understand where everyone falls on the bell curve of core virtues.

Observations by officers on the extreme ends of the bell curve—those representing either few core virtues or many core virtues—exert considerable influence on those who fall in the middle. Officers take note of the peers who hesitate to answer dispatched assignments, claim false injuries, sleep on duty, or have the habit of crossing the line in the use of excessive force. They know who tends to use demeaning language or profanity toward the public. They know who the brutal members are.

It is unfortunate, but when unethical practices aren't challenged by corporals, sergeants, and lieutenants, they become so normalized that some officers will engage in them, even though they know they are wrong. Take meals, for example. During morning and evening rush hour, which were always busy where I worked, units were prohibited from going out of service to eat. Yet in some sectors of the city, they did take meal breaks at these times, leaving fewer units available for calls. That resulted in delayed responses. With no challenges to these violations, it was a clear disservice to the public.

In some areas, it was accepted practice to punch a suspect who ran and was then caught after the foot chase. The tactic was rationalized. After a good punch, the suspect would not run again if approached by the police. When such low core value conduct is tolerated, officer behavior can easily become accepted practice. *They're getting away with it. Why can't I?* That behavior influences the performance of officers in the middle of the curve. Unfortunately, that's where most officers fall.

When racial slurs, profanity toward the public, quick fists, one too many baton strikes, and downright brutality become frequent and unpunished, observing officers' internal controls are subject to compromise. Frustrated and discouraged, they may begin to exhibit similar conduct, pushing the bell curve toward bad behavior. At a minimum, the officers in the middle of the bell curve will stop reporting the abuses they see—why should they go to the effort of reporting bad behavior if nothing is done? Without reporting, an essential tool for maintaining an ethical culture is lost.

Consider a platoon of one hundred officers where fifteen of them fall on the left side of the bell curve with few core virtues, seventy are closer to the middle with some core virtues, and fifteen officers land on the far right with many core virtues. If the fifteen officers on the lower end of the scale are never challenged or held accountable for unethical conduct, if they are never called to task, their numbers will grow because the central group of officers will give up. As that cohort expands, so will the weight of their influence on the others. Eventually, that platoon of one hundred officers could end up with forty officers exhibiting few core virtues, forty-five with some core virtues, and fifteen with many core virtues. Problems will escalate. By the time 40 percent of that platoon performs their duty with few core virtues, a culture of unethical conduct has taken root.

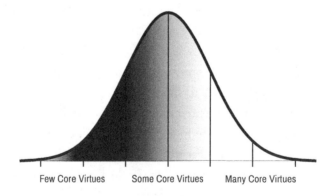

Few Core Virtues   Some Core Virtues   Many Core Virtues

Notice that the officers who fall on the upper end of the core virtue bell curve will always perform with integrity, no matter how others behave. Remember the story of NYPD officer Frank Serpico. If first-line supervisors and mid-level managers fail to hold subordinates on the lower end of the bell curve responsible for their actions, at minimum, it will result in mediocrity. At worst, it will result in major scandals, loss of public trust and confidence, civil suits, and criminal prosecutions of police officers.

To make a bad situation worse, those with strong core virtues—the most valuable members of the force—may get fed up with working in such a corrupt environment and leave. Star officers may request transfers to other assignments or quit an agency altogether. A police organization cannot afford to lose their most ethical officers.

That may sound bleak, but all is not lost. With deliberate effort, an undesirable culture can be transformed. By implementing a system that offers public recognition and rewards for high-performing members and forced, publicly witnessed accountability for low-performing members, first-line supervisors and mid-level managers have the power to influence behavior. Police officers who understand the value of integrity want to see those who behave unethically held responsible for their conduct. Remember the two officers I disciplined for calling out sick to go on a ski trip? Before that year was over, both officers, independently, came to my office and told me they were glad I had not let them get away with that behavior. Being held accountable had changed them. They became such outstanding police officers that they served as field training officers.

When officers observe supervisors responding to misconduct with swift action and hold offending officers accountable, they understand that bad behavior is unacceptable. Failing to respond to misconduct conveys an opposing message: the misdeed wasn't important and the behavior is acceptable.

If bad behavior is condemned and good behavior rewarded, most officers tend to move away from those who exhibit few core virtues and toward the ones who exhibit more. The behavioral baseline shifts. The one hundred officer platoon discussed earlier will now have ten officers with few core virtues, thirty with some core virtues, and sixty with many core virtues.

The culture of that squad, platoon, or section has been altered. Now, more officers are operating ethically in the performance of their duties:

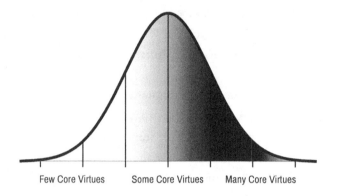

Few Core Virtues   Some Core Virtues   Many Core Virtues

Bell Curve Theory Impact

In the year 2000, the Los Angeles Police Department found the theory of the Police Core Virtue Bell Curve to be profound. Their 360-page Rampart Area Corruption Incident Board of Inquiry report stated that "mediocrity was alive and well in Rampart. . . . We are sad to report that we also found mediocrity threatening to engulf many of our other workplace environments as well. . . . Rather than challenging our people to do their best, too many of our leaders are allowing mediocre performance and, in some cases, even making excuses for it." This report agreed that corruption follows mediocrity.

I have presented the Police Core Virtue Bell Curve to many first-line supervisors in other agencies, including full-service sheriffs' departments. Student evaluations offered numerous positive comments: *this needs to be presented to the whole department; we need to do this right now; essential and much needed*; and *many can benefit from the excellent presentation*.

Implementing systems of accountability to encourage a higher standard of integrity requires tenacity and commitment. It means persistently watching for misbehavior and responding quickly and efficiently. It may hardly seem worth the effort to challenge an officer over the radio for being out of service too long or demanding the rewrite of a poorly prepared report, but these incidents should not be overlooked. Disciplining these minor infractions sends a strong message: officers are accountable for all their efforts. This, of course, may do little to instill core virtues in those on the low end of the scale, but it will have a significant impact on those in the middle. It creates a guidepost that instills confidence and trust in the supervisor. When officers trust the supervisor and are confident that all misconduct will be dealt with, they are more likely to manage their own behaviors and are certainly more willing to report misconduct among their peers.

No police organization can allow those with low core values to dominate its culture. In such circumstances, some officers are more likely to require higher levels of supervision to complete the tasks that others manage easily. Those same officers will take little initiative and, more often than not, do the minimum necessary to accomplish the job.

When those with high core virtues dominate the culture, officers are more likely to take the extra effort to do the right thing, use good judgment, be fair and judicious, practice self-control, and follow the rules and regulations of the department. As a result, officers share greater trust and confidence among themselves and with the general public for more responsible policing overall. The performance of officers with many core virtues can be contagious if the supervisors and mid-level managers create a climate to encourage them.

To be truly worthy of public trust, everyone within a police department must maintain an environment where it makes sense to behave with prudence, public trust, courage, intellectual honesty, justice, self-effacement of interests, and accountability. First-line supervisors and mid-level managers must ensure core virtues are established as visible, standard operating procedures (SOPs), and therefore, always present in the hearts and minds of those sworn to protect and serve. If they address the undesirable behavior of those on the lower end of the Police Core Virtue Bell Curve, they prevent mediocrity, improve the moral health of the department, and curb the kind of gross misconduct that shatters the trust and authority society has bestowed upon them.

The theory behind the bell curve is decades old, but its application is essential today. Importantly, this theory is not exclusive to the police. In my discussions with professionals in other fields such as airline pilots or firefighters, I repeatedly heard how well it applies to them too.

FOUR

Authority, Power, and Discretion

Police officers are entrusted by the public with unique authority and power. They have public permission and consent—or *authority*—to perform their duties, and they are equipped with the capability, capacity, and competence—or *power*—to do so. It is assumed they will use their power and authority wisely, and with discretion.

The Fundamentals

Two fundamentals are at work here. The first employs the social contract devised by British philosopher John Locke. In this contract, society gives up the right to personally enforce guarantees found in the Declaration of Independence. The second is the US Constitution, which passes that right to the government and, in particular, to the police. The police have the power in the performance of their duty to protect life, liberty, and property. As the late American sociologist Egon Bittner wrote in his book *The Functions of the Police in Modern Society*, published in 1970, the police are "a mechanism for the distribution of non-negotiable coercive force in accord with the dictates of an intuitive grasp of situational exigencies."[1] Bittner's studies of police work remain a benchmark for contemporary scholars and still alludes to force.[2]

What Bittner's words mean to me is that police have a special role in society. The police (the mechanism) handle urgent and emergency (exigencies) situations that only they have the authority to deal with and resolve because the situation may require the use of force. Their use of force is not open for debate or discussion (non-negotiable). The police using force is based on what they believe to be true (intuitive grasp) in accord with laws, rules, directives, principles to be obeyed (dictates).

So let's say a state trooper responds to a traffic accident involving two cars. The drivers of both vehicles have visible injuries, creating an *exigent* or emergency situation, although both are conscious and talking. The trooper calls for medical assistance and questions both drivers. One driver emits a strong odor of alcohol and slurs his words. There's an empty quart bottle of vodka on his front seat. Those factors lead the trooper to believe the driver is intoxicated.

With that *intuitive grasp* of the situation, the trooper places the driver under arrest for Driving While Intoxicated, according to the *dictate*, or governing law. When the arrested driver becomes aggressive and resists being handcuffed, the trooper assumes *non-negotiable use of coercive force*. He pushes the drunk up against his vehicle, forces his hands behind his back, and handcuffs him.

Some people believe that officers grapple daily with ethical concerns, a belief that may be inspired because of the discretion afforded to police officers and because there is little direct supervision of their performance. Each situation brings its own circumstances and may demand a different response. Officers answer calls for service, engage in self-generated police duties, and take assignments from superiors. Supervisors cannot be with their subordinates all the time. Therefore, officers must make decisions.

Officers well-versed in police core virtues and committed to exercising them don't grapple with ethical implications because they are prudent and skilled in good judgment. They apply ethical discretion instinctively and exercise impartial judgment and fairness in determining the rights of others according to the rules of law and equity. When they use discretion, they are responsible and able to answer for their conduct and obligations.

Discretion Scenarios

Every situation an officer encounters demands a series of decisions that test their discretion. For example, officers who observe a speeding car has a plethora of options. They can do nothing. They can attempt to stop the car. If the car attempts evasion, more options suddenly appear. They can pursue the car or not. If they choose to pursue, they can stop pursuit at some point or continue pursuit until its conclusion. If the car stops, the officers can ask for the operator's driver's license, registration, and proof of insurance.

That leads to more options. If the operator is not in possession of one of those required items, the officers can write a ticket, summarily make an arrest, offer a verbal warning, impound the car, or direct the driver not to operate the car. If officers stop the car and the driver has all the necessary items, they can issue a verbal warning, write a warning ticket or an actual ticket. Still more decisions. If officers smell alcohol on an operator's breath, they can ignore it, ask a few questions, or conduct a roadside breathalyzer test or a field sobriety test.

If probable cause indicates the operator is driving under the influence or driving while intoxicated, another list of possible decisions arises. Officers can let the operator go or call a friend or family member to pick them up. They can take the operator home or summarily make an arrest.

At some time and in some place, all of the aforementioned scenarios have occurred. Each scenario brings ethical implications that must be addressed at the discretion of the officer. An officer functioning with high core virtues will not grapple with these concerns. They will be confident and competent in their skills, knowledge and abilities to respond.

So why might an officer decide *not* to pursue a speeding car? Let's take a closer look at a few different scenarios.

Scenario #1

Officers allow the speeding car to pass and do nothing. It's 2 a.m. and they're focused on an all-night convenience store with only one clerk on duty. The area has recently experienced a rash of late-night robberies, and the officers just observed two men enter the store—one of whom is on parole for armed robbery. The convenience store issue is more pressing than the speeding car.

Scenario # 2

Officers attempt to pull the speeding car over, but it speeds away in an effort to elude the police. The officers do nothing. It's 3 p.m. in a high-density residential area. Students are being dismissed from the neighborhood elementary school and middle school, and school buses are everywhere. A high-speed pursuit could put lives at risk.

Police pursuits are dangerous under any circumstances, and with school children present in a residential neighborhood, it isn't a good idea. Such a pursuit is dangerous for the officers, for the operator of the fleeing vehicle, and, of course, for the public. An operator could lose control of the vehicle or strike pedestrians, or any number of other tragic outcomes could occur that could injure or kill or damage property.

Those are two fairly straightforward scenarios. What happens in a more complicated situation?

Scenario #3

A suspect runs away from the scene of a sexual assault as his accuser screams that he attacked her, despite the officers' call to stop. He then leaps into a vehicle and speeds away. The officers pursue him. It's 1 a.m., and the officers are aware that another marked patrol unit and a sergeant are on their way. They will soon arrive and attend to the victim. As the first officers engage in a vehicle pursuit, they advise the dispatcher and broadcast directions. A half mile later, the suspect crashes into a fire hydrant, exits his car, and begins running. Now what?

Possible response: pursue the suspect on foot or hold back. The officers broadcast their location and a full description of the suspect, pull their batons from the car, and make pursuit. As they close in, the suspect turns and charges.

Possible response: run from the suspect or apprehend him. The officers hear no backup in the immediate vicinity. With baton in hands, tasers, pepper spray and guns in their holsters, they choose not to run. The suspect leaps at an officer's throat.

Possible response: use taser, pepper spray, or gun—or strike the suspect with the baton. The officer strikes the suspect several times with the baton, breaking two of the suspect's ribs and a wrist. The attack stops, and the officer ceases to strike the suspect.

Later, an interview with the female complainant determines that she and the suspect were engaged in a domestic dispute. She was not assaulted. She told the emergency operator that she was being raped because she wanted the police to arrive faster.

Because of the use of force and resulting injuries, a question arises: Did the officer in question make ethical decisions? After the dust has settled, in the absence of all the facts and without a full understanding of the law, an observer or even a news reporter could state that the officer beat an unarmed man, resulting in two broken ribs and a broken wrist over a domestic dispute.

However, interpreting the law with all the facts in hand makes it clear that no ethical misconduct occurred in this incident. The officers had probable cause to arrest the suspect based on the complainant's initial report, and facts and circumstances presented—including the assault by the suspect.

Unfortunately, even with full understanding of the facts and the law, stories are sometimes spun to suggest the officer acted unethically. This kind of story is more likely to propagate when the public has lost trust in the police force, further inflaming mistrust in the police, and eroding public support and confidence. But if officers consistently perform within an ethical culture, they gain public trust. If ethical behavior is the norm, twisted reports tend to fall on deaf ears. In a culture built on police core virtues, encounters between the public and police are positive. If the encounters are positive and the public knows the police behave ethically, their experience and perception remain high regardless of what others may say or report. If police *fail* to perform their duty with core virtues, incidents such as those described above will inflame and mistrust in the police, eroding support and confidence.

Situations requiring discretion in police work are unavoidable, and they almost always have ethical implications. When force is used, discretion comes into the spotlight. If the force used is not applied with the ideology of police core virtues, issues arise—sometimes major issues.

If, as Bittner wrote, police are "a mechanism for the distribution of non-negotiable coercive force in accord with the dictates of an intuitive grasp of situational exigencies," who is making the decision to distribute non-negotiable coercive force? Who determines the dictates of an intuitive grasp of situational exigencies? Whose intuitive grasp of the situation is responsible for choosing a response? Through whose eyes is the situation an exigency? Who decides upon the level of force?

Obviously, the police are required to make those decisions. At each stage of intervention, they use discretion to arrive at those decisions. Therefore, it is essential that their credo, their central beliefs, and their reasoning are grounded in the police core virtues of prudence, trust, courage, intellectual honesty, justice, self-effacement of interests, and responsibility.

Here's another more complicated scenario of police discretion at work:

Scenario #4

Two officers stop a vehicle operating an in erratic fashion, braking and accelerating, weaving in and out of the oncoming lane. It is 1 a.m. One officer steps up to the driver's side window to question the operator, and another approaches the passenger side. They observe a nearly empty quart bottle of vodka on the seat next to the operator. As the operator is questioned, he responds with slurred words. The officers direct him to turn off the car, step out, and come to the sidewalk. The driver is administered a breathalyzer test that indicates he is intoxicated. One officer calls for a police transport while the other cuffs the driver's hands behind his back. A few minutes later, as the driver is escorted to the transport by one of the officers, he stomps on that officer's foot then spits in the officer's face, both painful and repugnant.

Possible response: ignore the apprehended driver's behavior or respond with equal or greater force. While a member of the general public might respond in kind, police officers are held to a higher standard. They must instinctively know if the situation at hand requires non-negotiable coercive force.

What is the officer's intuitive grasp of situational exigency? In an ethical police culture, three virtues come to mind: prudence, justice, and responsibility. Self-discipline and self-control are needed in the extreme. A righteous and a fair determination of rights according to the rule of law are also required. The officer must be responsible for his actions. In all likelihood, the officer is angry, agitated, and perhaps in pain. An officer who has self-control acts according to the rule of law and takes responsibility for his actions, using discretion. The officer stops with the suspect, slips a face mask on the suspect's face, and binds his legs at the knees—preventing a repeat of the incident—and continues walking the suspect to the transport vehicle where he is placed in the back.

In an ethical police culture, there is no retribution. There is no street justice administered. Officers are responsible for their behavior. If they were to respond with the use of excessive force, they would have to answer questions and explain why they struck a handcuffed prisoner.

Was this a trying experience for the officer? Of course! Still, the officer understands and believes in an ethical police culture and behaves accordingly. In a culture where ethical virtues are absent, another officer's drunken prisoner might have paid a visit to the hospital before being processed at the station house.

Because police are entrusted with authority, power, and discretion, it is imperative they hold to a high moral standard. Without a consistently reinforced ethical foundation, they will struggle with the quick and critical decisions they must make on every tour of duty. Some will often fail to make good decisions and risk corrupting the objectives that drove them to join the force in the first place.

FIVE

Corruption and the Noble Cause

Most police join the ranks to make a difference, to make the world a better and a safer place. Their moral and ethical value system drives them to serve, to protect the innocent and vulnerable. This is the *noble cause* of policing. Many officers have willingly sacrificed their lives for those they took an oath to protect.

What is *noble cause corruption*? It is the corruption of ethical policing that occurs when officers do bad things because they believe the outcomes will be good. It happens when police break the rules to protect innocent people by removing violent predators and criminals from the street as quickly as possible by whatever means necessary. They falsely believe that setting aside police core virtues, legal principles, and organizational policies for efficiency supports the noble cause, the good end. Noble cause corruption is *learned* behavior that becomes *accepted* behavior. It does not consider the importance of ethics-based policing.

We cannot pick and choose when we will obey rules, laws, and regulations.

The Gateway to Corruption

The academy doesn't teach rookies about the risks of corruption. It doesn't teach them about the slippery slope created when ethics are set aside. Recruits are still unaware of the risks when they join a police department and swear allegiance to the Constitution. Corruption is only learned through departmental culture. Rookies see it, adopt it, and either exercise it or ignore the use of it by others.

Often, rules are broken with good intentions, with public well-being in mind. That doesn't make the behavior appropriate. Each broken rule is a stepping stone toward further corruption. The longer that sergeants and lieutenants observe unethical behavior without responding, the wider the gateway opens to a full-blown ethical breakdown where anything goes. Accountability and responsibility vanish. Taking out the bad actors—the miscreants—by any means possible, becomes acceptable.

Metaphorically speaking, rule-breaking is a gateway drug. In a corrupt culture, performance is measured only in outcomes. Rewards and recognition are based on the number or importance of arrests made, or perhaps a letter from John Q. Citizen praising an officer's work. Results have powerful mojo—just what sergeants, lieutenants, and other superiors want to see. If these outcomes are achieved with no regard for *how*, there is a problem. Any hope of a prevailing ethical culture is shattered.

For instance, two officers make a traffic stop and tell the operator to get out of the vehicle. With no reasonable suspicion to prompt a search, one officer looks under the driver's seat and finds a pistol. In their reports, both officers share the same story: when one officer shined his flashlight into the car, he saw in plain view a pistol on the floor near the operator's feet. Good ends were achieved (an illegal gun was seized) by bad means (an illegal search and falsifying the police report). In an ethical culture, both the means and the ends or outcomes are of equal importance.

Now, consider the same case with different means. Two officers make the traffic stop of the same car and operator. They *ask permission* to search the car and the operator says, "Of course." They find the pistol under the seat. Good ends (a gun off the street) and good means (consent for the search).

How can this happen and why? Sergeants and other mid-level police officials are well aware of their subordinates' behavior. In an unethical culture, at best, they tolerate it. At worst, they encourage it. Either way, their response reflects their own deviation from police core virtues. Curiously, however, if you were to ask anyone involved—the officials or the officers—most will tell you that the unethical behavior is conducted for a *good reason*. It reflects their commitment to serve the public and a determination to be more effective in their duties, so they can quickly incarcerate violent, dangerous criminals. The unethical behavior is viewed as a tool for fighting against crime to support the public they serve.

My experience is this: cops who are brutal behave that way for a reason. They are administering what they feel is justice. Their rationale? The bad actor deserves it. The courts aren't going to do anything, so their actions are justified. They'll teach the bad actor a lesson that will prevent future bad behavior. They believe their actions offer retribution and vengeance against individuals who are hurting the people police have sworn to protect.

After studying hundreds of recruits' psychiatric evaluations through the screening process, I can say that 90 percent of the people entering the police service have a strong sense of right and wrong. They are predisposed to seek the right, the good, to triumph over evil. They enter the police force to pursue what they consider to be the noble cause of justice and the good ends of taking criminals off the streets.

In society, the spectrum of what defines good ends is wide. A monetary fine, restitution, probation, incarceration, or revocation of some privileges for an offender might be deemed sufficient. But in police service, the spectrum is usually far narrower. A police officer may only view incarnation of an offender as good ends. As stated earlier, the good ends are to remove very bad people from society, to incarcerate violent, dangerous men, and to serve and protect the public. Rookie police officers, straight out of the academy, already possesses a strong sense of right and wrong and are likely to follow the rules. If they enter a police culture where the ends justify the means, however, their perception of right and wrong behavior is slowly whittled away.

As rookies interact with citizens who are generally good people, they listen. The public expresses their need for police to slash crime and violence so they can live without the resulting fear and disorder. They can do nothing about these issues, but the police can, and they don't care how the situation is corrected. They just want to be safe.

Rules are bent, shortcuts taken, and written orders and procedural practices are disregarded, all in pursuit of good ends. If rookies aren't held accountable for these ethical breaches, and if no one else in the department is held accountable for ethical failures, rookies quickly lose sight of police core virtues. Their focus is shifted toward achieving what they deem to be satisfactory outcomes. Now the recruit finds themselves possessing a strong sense of right and wrong in a results-driven culture. Moral dilemmas arise. Where and how do they draw the line between acceptable and unacceptable behavior?

The noble cause forms the heart of police culture. It inspires values and animates daily work routines. If police officers are so moved by the noble cause that they are willing to do anything to achieve so-called good ends, they have corrupted their profession. If their behavior is ignored or encouraged by superiors, then those superiors have also corrupted the profession. They've all received the wrong message about the noble cause of policing and become part of the problem, not the solution.

This corruption has consequences. At some point, a police department or unit willing to break the rules will lose legitimacy with the public it serves. Then everyone suffers. A lack of public trust interferes with cooperation between citizens and the police, and that hampers the ability of the police to do their job protecting and serving the public.

Breaking the rules and discarding police core virtues serves no one well. No amount of rationalizing can change unethical police conduct into something noble and just. Planting evidence, "testa-lying" (committing perjury), illegal searches, coerced confessions, and "street justice" are wrong. Sooner or later, there are consequences, always bad. As public support for and confidence in the police falls, additional controls are instituted. The best and brightest police officers abandon the profession until only those who fall on the wrong side of police core virtues remain. Some officers are criminally charged. The media goes on a feed-ing frenzy. Morale tanks and heads roll. Police become short-staffed. Budgets are cut. Investigations are initiated and public hearings take place. These consequences devastate police departments, the profession, and the public, who is no longer adequately served.

Decades ago, the film *Dirty Harry*, starring Clint Eastwood, de-picted a San Francisco homicide detective, Harry Callahan. He was notorious for the unorthodox, violent, and ruthless methods he used against the criminals and killers he was assigned to apprehend. Recall the Smith and Wesson, Model 29, .44 magnum revolver he carried and made famous. *Dirty Harry's* approach to criminal justice was so popular that several sequels to the film were made. It was a hit with those in the trade. I enjoyed it too—but I recognized it as entertainment, a movie, and not real. That was *not* the way the men and women I worked with did business.

In the original movie, Callahan seizes custody of a kidnapper by shooting him in the leg. The kidnapper buried his victim alive, and only he knows where to find her. He won't divulge the location, and time is short. Callahan presses for answers by stepping on the perpetrator's bullet wound and grinding it to create pain. Although the victim is eventually found, they're too late. She's dead. The case against the per-petrator falls apart because of the means Callahan used against him.

This fictional scenario raises important questions reflected in real life—questions that test the corruption of the noble cause:

1. How does Callahan's approach defeat justice and poison the idea of a noble cause?
2. Can you think of any circumstances where the ends might justify the means, and if so, what are they?
3. What happens to the value of the law when law enforcement doesn't abide by the regulations designed to govern its behavior?

As you can see, using dirty means—even with good intentions—is risky, and it's impossible to know in advance whether good ends will be achieved. So what happens in the *Dirty Harry* case after using any means to achieve the noble end?

1. The suspect goes free because the evidence is inadmissible; the police violated the rights of the prisoner in custody.
2. Even though the victim ultimately dies, the crime for which the perpetrator was charged can no longer be prosecuted because police violated his legal rights.
3. Once the suspect is set free and turned loose on society, he continues to prey on the innocent.

Callahan cannot possibly determine the outcome of his actions. No matter how brutal his interrogation, there is always the chance that the perpetrator will lie. He may lie to buy time for an accomplice, to place blame on someone else, to reflect a complete lack of conscience regarding the crime, or, as a sociopath, to take pleasure in outwitting the police.

Aggressive tactics don't work for other reasons too. Perhaps the suspect doesn't know the information being sought. What is the sense in using dirty means if there is no guarantee that the intended goals will be achieved? Are there any other options? Of course! In the *Dirty Harry* case, legal methods of interrogation may have succeeded. They had at least as much potential as illegal ones. Experienced detectives can get cooperation and information from even the most hardened criminals with scrupulous attention to detail as well as intelligent and practiced interrogation techniques based on an understanding of human psychology. They do so without the risk of losing admissibility of evidence and without compromising their integrity.

Warrior Mentality

Not only does Harry Callahan depict corruption of the noble cause, but his behavior touches on another possible result of an unethical police culture: development of a warrior mentality. In many places across this nation, particularly in large metropolitan areas, there are bad actors—

truly violent people who will attack or kill at the drop of the hat. They prey upon the innocent whom the police are sworn to protect and serve, and sometimes, they prey upon police officers themselves. Anytime officers go on duty, they risk encountering violence or even death regardless of whether they serve in a large city or a small one.

Under these conditions, fairly well depicted by *Dirty Harry*, some officers adopt a warrior mentality. That kind of ideology creates ethical issues in the performance of duty. Police officers are not warriors. The general public is not their enemy. Officers are protectors, peacekeepers, and service providers. They are not trained to engage in battle while on tour of duty, and they are not expected to engage in battle. When they do encounter violent offenders, it is their duty to use the minimum force necessary to stop the violence, not to dispense punishment. Violent predators must be pursued relentlessly and brought to justice, but they must be taken into custody without excessive force and brutality.

Some academics find that fear motivates a lot of excessive force.[1] Defensive tactics are taught at the academy, but the skills aren't always maintained. That leaves some officers unsure about how to use defensive strategies in violent situations. Ed Maguire, a professor at the Arizona State University School of Criminology and Criminal Justice, told *Courier* that in such situations, "Fear is motivating a lot of excessive force because you just have a lot of officers out there who don't know how to handle themselves properly." He also said, "We don't talk enough about fear and its driving force in terms of excessive use of force, but we have human beings out there who are really concerned about being able to go home safely at the end of the day and they're scared about whether they're going to be injured or killed. . . . Fear is motivating a lot of excessive force . . ."

Faced with daunting challenges, some police officers adopt a warrior mindset in order to mask their fear, according to Seth Stoughton, a professor of law at the University of South Carolina and a former police officer. Stoughton goes on to say in the *Harvard Law Review* in 2016 that "they are taught that they live in an intensely hostile world. A world that is, quite literally, gunning for them."[2] This instills fear in officers who respond by being hypervigilant and treating every individual they interact with as an armed threat and every situation as a deadly force encounter in the making.

The findings of Maguire and Stoughton differ from my experience, which clearly shows that the warrior mentality ferments in a police culture lacking ethical core values. After leading or reviewing many investigations into alleged police use of excessive force, I discovered that fear on the part of the accused officer was never a motivating factor. Make no mistake: police work is dangerous. Still, in four decades on the job, I found no evidence that officers believed the communities they served were "gunning for them." I have never encountered an officer who could work tours of duty, week after week and month after month, in the type of hypervigilant state such a belief would induce.

The thousands of officers I worked with knew fear, but they had courage. Fear, hypervigilance, supposed warrior training—none of those factors led to use of excessive force. The cause always circled back to a police culture without ethical grounding, without responsible supervisors, without accountable subordinates. First-line supervisors and mid-level managers permitted a lackadaisical culture to take root. Within a weak cultural construct, a warrior mentality can grow, and if it is not immediately checked by the first-line supervisor or lieutenant, it can spread and intensify like a virus. When police core virtues are not upheld, rogue cops emerge.

A rogue cop believes the badge is a license to dispense justice, a license to injure or inflict maximum harm at the slightest provocation. Violence is extended toward everyone and anyone. Some rogue cops inflict harm on those who have done nothing more than violate the Rogue Cop Code by showing Contempt of Cop, which could be evoked by even the slightest sign of disrespect. Rogue officers believe they are always right. They have no allies beyond their fellow officers because only their fellow officers can truly understand the job or the challenges they face. Anyone who is not an officer is a potential enemy. Rogue cops tend to lose self-control in physical altercations. Some even seek confrontation by baiting others into situations that allow them to exercise their faulty warrior ideology. I have seen this firsthand. In fact, I have been a victim of such conduct.

Well, maybe not exactly a victim.

The following incident took place when I was in civilian clothes driving home in my own vehicle during rush hour in a large metropolitan city. As I approached a flashing yellow traffic light on a major artery, I noticed a marked scout car sitting on the intersecting street facing a flashing red traffic signal. I slowed, proceeding with caution. The scout car zipped out in front of me, apparently without looking, causing me to slam the brakes to avoid a collision. In frustration and alarm, I shrugged my shoulders and raised my hands in "a what was that all about?" gesture.

Of course, the officer saw my gesture in his rearview mirror. I had committed Contempt of Cop. His reaction was swift and sure. He stopped his car in the intersection, lit up his emergency lights, rolled down his widow, and signaled for me to do the same. He yelled out the window, "Don't you know you are supposed to stop?"

Of course, I couldn't help myself. "YOU had the red light," I yelled back. As soon as the words left my mouth, I knew I'd done it.

The officer slid out of his car. He came to my window and asked for my driver's license and registration, which I gave him. He then proceeded to lecture me like an errant child: I was supposed to stop.

Never adverse to confronting such conduct, I explained to him that under the city's municipal regulations, Title 18 of the Traffic Code section so and so, part III A, it says, "When approaching a flashing yellow light, one should slow and proceed with caution and when approaching a flashing red light, one should stop and proceed only when it is clear."

Since we were a block from the police station house, I informed him we could continue this discussion with Commander Greene in her office—she'd worked for me when she was a lieutenant—and we could review the officer's apparent lack of knowledge regarding traffic laws.

The officer handed back my permit and registration. "No, that won't be necessary. Have a good evening." He departed quickly.

The situation irritated me, but I had the experience and authority to deal with it. I can only imagine the distaste such an encounter would have left with the average citizen.

On another occasion, I attended a tailgate gathering at a large university football game. Students were enjoying themselves and doing nothing unlawful, but pairs of college police officers marched around wearing aggressive expressions and growling their authority with aggressive statements such as "What are you looking at?" and "I'll lock you up."

I was disturbed and disappointed by their behavior, which did little but alienate their constituents. These officers had bought into the warrior ideology. Students were the enemy, and these officers were looking for the slightest provocation to turn on them.

The same attitude is apparent at an ocean resort I often visit. The resort police treat the young folks there as though they are hardened criminals by assaulting them with profanity and baiting them into confrontations. Even the slightest noncompliance is met with over-the-top force.

I am a follower of Edmund Burke, an Irish statesman and philosopher who served as a member of parliament in the late eighteenth century in the House of Commons in Great Britain. He once said, "The only thing necessary for the triumph of evil is for good men to do nothing." That may be true, but reacting when there is no evil afoot, as the cops at the traffic light and the tailgate party had, is wrong. There must be evil for good men to act. As previously noted, in Egon Bittner's book *The Functions of the Police in Modern Society*, he states, "Police are a mechanism for the distribution of non-negotiable coercive force in accord with the dictates of an intuitive grasp of situational exigencies."[3] But there must be situational exigencies—emergencies—for the distribution of non-negotiable coercive force.

When their behavior is not informed by the police core virtues of prudence, trust, courage, intellectual honesty, justice, self-effacement of interest, and responsibility, officers will fail. Excessive force will increase, and brutality will take place. Corporals, sergeants, and lieutenants must create and maintain an operational culture that instills core virtues, demands that core virtues are always exercised, and holds every office accountable for their actions.

This approach thwarts the warrior mentality. It eliminates demeaning language, brutality, use of excessive force, and other acts of misconduct against citizens. At the same time, it creates a high-performing, effective, efficient, and dedicated police force, because those same values are applied to every aspect of police work. It creates a high level of integrity that ensures responsibilities are carried out thoroughly and with integrity. It prevents corner cutting, violations of fundamental civil liberties and laws, violations of oaths of office, abuses of authority and power—all acts that betray the public trust.

When the warrior mentality is taken care of, every aspect of questionable and illegal behavior is addressed. Rookies entering the law enforcement arena with a strong sense of right and wrong are supported by their constituents, peers, and superiors. They're steeped in an ethical culture and the noble cause is upheld.

Criminal Investigations and the Noble Cause

Means-ends conflicts create corrupting situations and present profound moral dilemmas in every level of law enforcement. While this book thus far has focused on building an ethical culture among uniformed patrol officers, police core virtues are just as critical among investigators and detectives. Detectives have as much responsibility for adhering to professional standards and ethical behavior as anyone else in the police force. Unethical acts among detectives occur through acts of commission and omission, just as they do in uniform patrol: doing what they are not supposed to do and not doing what they should do.

In 2001, county homicide detectives in Maryland reportedly coerced confessions and denied suspects lawyers during marathon interrogations. These practices appear to violate state rules and exceed bounds set by other police agencies, according to a yearlong investigation by the *Washington Post*. Four men were detained in the interrogation room from eleven to thirty-eight hours. Three of the four insisted that detectives refused to let them speak with a lawyer. In each case, the suspect's alleged statement was virtually the only evidence homicide detectives used to charge them with murder. In two of the cases, the trail went cold while police focused on what prosecutors eventually concluded was the wrong man. This allowed the true killer to remain at large. In all four cases, homicide detectives misread, ignored, or lost evidence and failed to follow significant leads, records, and interviews.

Various newspapers reported that in each case, the suspect was only exonerated through the intervention of outsiders, such as detectives from other units, savvy lawyers, and crime lab experts. The investigating detectives corrupted the noble cause by trying to close cases quickly and targeting potential suspects without a thorough investigation—unethical conduct committed for what they considered good ends.

Similar to patrol officers who engage in noble cause corruption, some detectives have good intentions. They want to rid our streets of violent predators, reduce or eliminate the pain and suffering of the innocent, protect the law-abiding public, and see that offenders are brought to justice. They are moral men and women, acting in an uncertain world to bring about a noble end. But where and how do they draw the line between acceptable and unacceptable conduct in order to reach the noble end? How big a step is it for detectives to corrupt the noble cause if they're working in a legal framework that permits deception and lying to obtain confessions?

Criminal investigations traditionally hold an air of mystique in the eyes of the public and uniform police officers. Their realm is strictly crime-focused, "real police business." They are tenacious specialists who will doggedly pursue offenders and bring them to justice. When the "suits" show up, confusion dissipates, confidence is gained, and everything is under control. At least, that is the perception. The respect garnered by this mystique is by no means a bad thing. However, when a thin veil of secrecy about how and what they do carries over to operations, the door to unethical behavior is opened. The mystical cloak worn by detectives is a double-edged sword.

On a slow night with no other incidents, a fifty-five-minute response time by detectives to a critical shooting seems long. Doesn't that warrant a challenge? When detectives located in the office are unresponsive to patrol officers' requests for assistance at a crime scene, does that not also warrant a challenge? When a detective arrives on the scene clearly under the influence of alcohol, does that not warrant a challenge? These are not rhetorical or hypothetical questions. They're based on actual incidents where ethically responsible oversight is missing. Police officials, investigative and uniform, have a positional duty and a moral obligation to provide oversight.

When I served as a captain, one of the officers in my unit was involved in an exchange of gunfire with a bad actor. Fortunately, the officer escaped injury, but the gunman was wounded and transported to the hospital under guard. The homicide detectives and I arrived at the crime scene. Tasked with investigating all police-involved shootings whether fatal or not, the detectives started interviewing the few witnesses present. I asked one of the detectives to go to the hospital to interview the gunman.

This detective turned to me with a look of disdain. "Captain, you know very well the gunman won't say a word," he replied, with a condescending tone.

His arrogance, his assumptions, and his disregard for protocol irritated me. "Detective," I replied with an even voice, "unlike you, I did not consult Ms. Cleo from the psychic hotline prior to my tour of duty, and I failed to read the gunman's palm before he left the scene. So, no. I do not know that he won't say a word. I am giving you a direct order: you can personally carry yourself directly to the hospital and interview that shooter."

I later learned, no less from the detective I ordered to the hospital, that the shooter readily gave a full confession.

Sometimes detectives corrupt the noble cause in more personal ways—to protect themselves. On March 23, 2009, a special agent with the FBI in Phoenix pleaded guilty to a trio of wire fraud charges. Let's call him Graham. The charges were related to Graham's improper sexual relationship with the wife of a man he investigated in two separate matters. Graham sought a favorable plea agreement for his mistress' husband to convince him not to disclose Graham's indiscretion. Graham contacted prosecutors and successfully argued that the husband should receive a reduced sentence. In doing so, Graham compromised at least two criminal investigations.[4]

In other cases, corruption runs deeper. In June of 2013, the infamous Boston mobster, Whitey Bulger, went to trial accused of numerous crimes, including nineteen murders, and running a criminal enterprise with the help of the FBI. The testimony of an FBI agent spotlighted a staggering amount of corruption in the Boston FBI field office that included cash bribes and tip-offs to wiretaps. The behavior of the crooked agents did not raise any eyebrows with the Special Agents in Charge of the Boston FBI field office said an agent.[5]

The conduct of supervisors and managers must sustain not only the departmental code of ethics, but the individual characters of the people who serve there. Even when men and women are virtuous, even when they behave with high standards of conscience, responsible supervision and continuously conveyed expectations for high moral behavior encourages that behavior. If supervisors and managers do not show that they take ethics seriously, their agency codes will be treated as worthless platitudes.

Detectives are not bestowed with ethics and integrity at the moment they are pinned with a gold shield. Supervisory control, ethical supervision, and training are essential and must be ongoing. As with police officers, it is the first line of defense against unethical behavior. It is the only way law enforcement can provide an external moral compass for detectives to make ethical judgments in line with the investigative function and the organization.

Supervisory issues influencing the ethical culture of an investigative unit are similar to those governing police patrols, even though the types of duties are different. One of those issues concerns how vacancies in the detective grade are filled. Detectives should be selected based on merit. Experience, training, skill, dedication, ethical conduct, and test scores should be considered. Cronyism should not play a role. Selecting detectives according to loyalty or "good old boys' club" membership is inconsistent with basic tenants of truth, professionalism, and moral responsibility. Not only does this send the wrong message to others aspiring for detective positions, but it is a disservice to the department and the public.

What goes for selecting detectives also applies to making assignments and evaluating performance. Performance evaluations should not be rubber stamped, boilerplate productions. They should accurately reflect the caliber of a detective's work, outline areas requiring correction or improvement, and annotate superior work if appropriate.

Another management ethical issue concerns the longevity of investigative assignments. Detectives should be held accountable for their performance. For example, if a detective assigned to a homicide squad does not perform well or works poorly with the public, there must be consequences. On the other hand, if detectives perform with a high level of competency and integrity and suit a particular investigative position, they become experts in their field and a valuable resource to the public and their police department. These men and women are assigned the toughest cases and generally hold their assignments for years.

When I ran homicide in DC, I kept my best detectives assigned to the Cold Case Squad for many years, and they closed many murders that had been unsolved for a decade or more. One detective in that homicide unit performed without any sense of urgency and was not up to the standards necessary for homicide investigations. With some difficulty, I managed to transfer that detective to another position. Other detectives with alcohol problems were transferred out of general crimes investigations and back to uniform patrol where they could receive closer supervision.

Just as assignments should be based on performance, so should rewards—even small ones. Although many institutions base rewards for service on longevity, *performance*—not longevity—should be the determining factor. When more attractive days off became available, I assigned them to top-performing detectives, not to the detectives who were around the longest. That conveyed the expectation of performance as the driving force in the unit.

Corruption of the noble cause is fueled by the unwillingness of some supervisors to take on the challenge of ethics-based policing, but as part 1 has clearly shown, ethics-based policing is the only way to polish the tarnished reputation of policing and ensure it continues to be an honorable profession. If the corporals, sergeants, and lieutenants uphold this responsibility, ethics-based policing will succeed, and a sea change will follow.

PART TWO

Implementing Change

SIX

Synergy in the Police Force

Part 1 outlined the elements of an ethical police force culture. Part 2 shares deeper insight into establishing that culture and addresses measures for attaining it. As noted in part 1, it is ultimately the responsibility of supervisors to create and sustain the culture by holding their subordinates accountable for their actions. But there is more.

When supervisors are deliberate and consistent in creating and sustaining an ethical culture and their charges step on board, something else happens. Synergy emerges. Through the power of synergy, the police force entity becomes greater than the sum of its parts—the ultimate goal of ethics-based policing. As more and more members of a department actively participate in ethical practices, increasingly higher standards are achieved. Higher standards inspire new initiatives. Goals are achieved more rapidly because everyone is moving in the same direction.

Consider a police force with one hundred carefully recruited officers and detectives. When an ethical culture is established and synergy takes hold, the force is not just one hundred officers and detectives who behave ethically. The force actually becomes one hundred officers and detectives who create new ethical approaches to their work. Eventually, that behavior compounds and spreads to the wider community. The wider community is increasingly compelled to trust the police and to participate in a culture that extends far beyond the walls of the department.

In this environment of synergistic, ethics-based policing, use of excessive force is reduced or eliminated. The community is treated with dignity and respect—even the bad actors. No more profanity or demeaning language is used. Retribution, payback, vengeance, street justice, and use of excessive force have no place. As police effort, dedication, and commitment become more evident, residents observe the change. Seeing is believing. They begin to view officers as kind, caring, empathic individuals who are responsive to their needs. Respect between the police and their community grows.

A synergistic relationship between the police and the public they serve is essential. But it takes a lot to get there. Many police agencies are currently in a bad way. Morale is low. This once-honorable profession experiences continual assault from the media, the general public, and politicians. No one in the rank and file is happy with the current situation, including first-line supervisors and mid-level managers. Something needs to change, but it won't change until there is a greater sense of urgency for tackling the foundation of ethics and establishing ethics-based policing. It *is* attainable, but first, leadership must buy in.

Supervisor Buy-In

Developing synergy by implementing a change to police force culture requires action from those in supervisory positions. Everyone in a position of authority needs to step up—from the commissioner and chief of police down to the corporals, sergeants, and lieutenants who supervise officers and detectives. They must lead the way for ethical behavior from their subordinates. If they aren't doing what they are supposed to do, or if they're doing what they are *not* supposed to do, now is the time to change. They must adjust their outlook, boost their skill levels, and improve their methods of supervision and communication. These changes will only come about when those in authority recognize they have the power to influence change and accept the responsibility to do so.

Reactions to the concepts I'm about to present will vary among subordinates, so in most cases, the ranking police official selected as trainer must be prepared to take the bull by the horns. The most suitable person for the role is someone who has "cred" with their subordinates and is one hundred percent on board, someone who is respected by superiors, peers, and subordinates and knows how to get things done.

Even with the right man or woman at the helm, it won't be easy. Several stages are involved. Some steps can be taken immediately to reap significant change to the ethical culture. Other steps are longer term in nature, but they will create deeper improvements to police culture and establish a maintenance program. A few members of the force will buy in right away. Others will resist because any change means thwarting the existing culture.

In chapter 2, I described how a cohort of fifteen experienced officers *unanimously* identified the lack of discipline as the most serious issue facing police departments. Too many officers got away with too much. They expected supervisors to consistently hold officers accountable for their conduct.[1] In my experience, with consistency and determination, effective leadership transforms resistance into buy-in.

A score of police agencies reviewed the analysis and tactics this book describes and several agencies implemented them. The Los Angeles Police Department adopted my work in response to the Rampart Division Corruption Report, which stated that rather than challenging people to do their best, "too many of our leaders are allowing mediocre performance and, in some cases, even making excuses for it."[2] I presented my work to other departments too. Evaluations from those who attended included annotations such as "This class needs to be presented to all sergeants and lieutenants"; "The whole department needs to hear this"; and "Well-done presentation . . . knows what he is talking about, important and essential."

All police agencies, even ones currently running well, can benefit from a sharper focus on ethical standards. That means creating a program or an initiative to train and educate corporals, sergeants, and lieutenants about their roles in maintaining or building an ethical police culture. Obviously, those who find themselves in a bad way will gain the most.

Ethics-based policing must first be introduced to department executives. Their support and input for program development is essential. Recommendations, guidance, and opinions from above will enhance the initiative's legitimacy and ensure that it moves forward with urgency. Introducing the strategy to high-level managers requires some planning by the executive. A mandatory training curriculum to introduce the concepts could bring them on board. Such a curriculum would begin by reviewing the analysis outlined in part 1 to help them more clearly see the problem and their role in addressing it.

Some supervisors will welcome the new direction and view the responsibility as a breath of fresh air. Others may be receptive, although the current state of their department may cause some skepticism. Still others will buck change. Those who resist may have seen other initiatives come and go with little or no results. They may not like or agree with ethics-based policing for whatever reason—such as the laissez-faire supervisor now required to do some work. Others may feel that the system is working well already or feel anxious about new strategies or any change in general.

Supervisor reaction depends on the existing ethical culture. Some departments may have to build ethics-based policing from the ground up. Other departments may find significant improvement by simply tuning up good processes already in place. Be that as it may, change is never easy. Where complacency, mediocrity, unethical conduct, and rule-breaking are accepted norms, more time, effort, and dedication will be necessary. If the department has a history of failed efforts toward change, such as the adoption of community policing, directed patrol programs, problem-oriented policing applications, or community outreach plans, garnering support for value-based policing will meet more skepticism and resistance.

The entire process will have more credibility if the selected trainer is or has been one of them, a supervisor of patrol officers with rank. If not, some members of the ranks will rightfully resist. Comments like "You don't know what it is like out there" or "You don't know what you are talking about, so what you say is useless" are to be expected.

In the early 1980s, a new performance evaluation process was introduced by a captain with little line experience and lots of time behind an administrative desk. Most line police officials identified the new process as time-consuming and ineffective. Questions and doubts concerning its viability were openly presented to the captain, who was unable to address their concerns. Undeterred, the captain told them that the process was going to happen whether they liked it or not, and they would just have to do it. The new evaluation process lasted six months. Ultimately, it was abandoned.

Experience has sway. I spent my career in line positions never seeking nor working in an administrative assignment. When I addressed or guided subordinate police officials, they listened. They understood my message, and they followed my directions. They trusted me because I had decades of line assignments under my belt, both patrol and investigative. They knew that I knew what I was talking about.

It's essential that supervisors understand they are the linchpins for change. The agency, the public, and their officers require their help. Without their career-long commitment to the men and women they lead, without their dedication to creating and sustaining ethics-based policing, matters will only change for the worse. Empower these supervisors. Help them understand the good that will come from creating an ethical culture. Help them see their value, ability, and responsibility to achieve this end.

Those who present the ethical, value-based approach to change must persevere in changing hearts. They must convince, cajole, entertain, understand, empathize, reward, and, if necessary, use carefully placed threats to get the program rolling. If they fail to bring supervisors on board, the status quo stands—and the status quo is unacceptable. Just ask your supervisors if they are happy with the way things are.

At one point in my policing career, I developed and implemented a new process for promoting people within the department. Prior to this, promotions were mostly a popularity contest—no test, no oral board, no review of performance. Commitment and dedication meant little. When I announced the change during a staff meeting, a sergeant and lieutenant looked down and shook their heads. They had been promoted the old way.

At the end of the staff meeting, I asked the attendees for help. I needed their feedback and critical analysis of my progress. I named the hesitant sergeant and lieutenant as my right-hand man and woman. I brought them into the midst of the change, and the program's success was in no small part due to their participation. Shortly after coming on board, they were singled out for attention. They recognized the benefits the program would bring to the department, and they were eager to see it succeed. Potential naysayers can become surprising change agents if they are invited to assist in the process.

In another scenario, I implemented a police vehicle inspection form to be filled out each time an officer used a police vehicle. This inspection reported any new damage, the fuel level, any mechanical issues, and the cleanliness of the vehicle, and accounted for all equipment. The form was to be turned into a sergeant at the end of each tour of duty for review.

One sergeant complained, "That's all we need. More paperwork."

I caught up with him a few days later and asked if he remembered taking over a police vehicle from another officer when he was an officer. He said he did.

"Did you ever take over a police car that was dirty, with a flat spare, a quarter tank of gas, or a burned-out headlight?" I asked.

"Well, yes."

"Were you disturbed to be stuck with a police car in that condition?"

"More than disturbed." He grinned. "I see your point."

Sometimes a little explanation goes a long way. Since that particular change was instituted, sergeants are now responsible to holding their subordinates accountable for ensuring their squad cars are in good condition when they complete their tour of duty.

Finding the Best Recruits

Of course, ethics-based policing also requires close attention to the quality of men and women recruited to join the force. Recommendations from some members of the public, legislators, and media suggest that adding members from a certain gender or race would create a more balanced representation of society within the police force. They suggest it could also contribute to a reduction in the use of excessive force. Although the idea has some merit, implementing such a mandate is a daunting task. It further minimizes the pool of available, qualified candidates for reasons we'll get into shortly. Other solutions proposed include testing applicants for bias, implementing mechanisms to determine the level of threat that triggers an applicant's aggression, and testing for empathy, impulse control, paranoia, and independent thinking. But more than 90 percent of law enforcement agencies in the United States *already* require psychological screening of their applicants.[3]

Even without such specifications, finding recruits with the best potential for policing has always been a challenging proposition. Police departments have high standards for those they accept. Finding recruits who meet those high standards and also *want* to become police officers are two high hurdles to overcome. The search is time consuming, costly, and complicated. Recruiting tactics are broad. They include radio and newspaper ads, posters, job fairs, the internet, and word of mouth. The results of these scattershot methods have been mediocre at best. As more and more departments seek candidates with higher levels of education, the situation becomes increasingly difficult. In my experience, applicants' strong ethical grounding best determines their success in serving the public.

When I led a medium-sized department—160 sworn—we experienced minimal turnover, but retirements and departmental expansion necessitated increased hiring. Previously, we had posted invitations for application on the federal job website. Opening an ad for just a week resulted in hundreds of applications, and, of course, many hours of screening to separate out those who met the basic qualifications. Many did not.

Because we required candidates to have a post-secondary education, we also attended job fairs at colleges and universities. We competed with a number of other agencies, had little time to talk to interested graduating seniors, and incurred significant expenses. Each job fair cost up to one thousand dollars simply to register as a job fair participant. Additional costs included travel, officer time, a per diem for department representatives, and more. Although we handed out plenty of applications, few were returned. The results were less than impressive.

There had to be a better way to find and hire the very best candidates. Success struck when I tried an experiment—not subjective success, but empirically proven success. It began as an effort to measure and compare methods for recruiting and hiring the best people for the job by selectively inviting candidates *in* rather than screening them *out*. We would approach post-secondary institutions directly to address a narrow field of interested candidates and then narrow that field further.

First, we identified a group of ten officers who would best represent the department. In addition to being outgoing, personable, engaging, and physically and mentally fit, they loved the job and recognized the importance of the mission they were about to embark on. They were asked to contact the dean or professors from their alma maters to propose the possibility of meeting with graduating students. Two officers would spend an hour speaking with students about the profession of policing and then meet with interested parties one-on-one or in small groups for further discussion.

To guide the officers in their presentations, I drafted a ten-page document listing all the aspects of our department they should convey. Many potential candidates only know police work from what they have seen on television or perhaps from talking to others. A few may have participated in a ride along with an on-duty officer. While all departments are there to protect and serve, levels of service vary widely across the country. Policing in a big city is different from policing a county sheriff's department in rural Idaho. It was my goal to see that potential recruits were informed about all the duties and responsibilities of the department: the challenges, training, risks, rewards, benefits, and the expectations we had of them.

For example, recruits to my department would be trained in dignitary protection; active shooter response; nuclear, biological, and chemical attack response; and criminal laws. They would be drilled about these tactics and encounter other training opportunities, both required and optional, throughout their career. Because my department was small and could not afford teams dedicated to specific duties, officers were expected to become experts in many aspects of police work that other departments typically assigned to single-task officers. While some departments might engage emergency response teams to overcome a gunman, for example, every officer in my department was periodically trained to perform that duty.

The group of officer representatives were divided into diverse teams generally consisting of a male and a female officer, one in uniform and one in plain clothes. Teams rehearsed their presentations before me or the police official supervising them. That way, we could provide constructive feedback before they gave their presentations to potential recruits. Because I didn't know how the new strategy would compare to the two methods we were already using—widespread advertising and posting on the federal job site—I created a matrix to capture all the information and measure the results.

RECRUITMENT STEPS	RECRUITMENT STRATEGY		
	INTERNET	JOB FAIR	SELECTIVE INVITATION
1. Passed HR screening	83	17	13
2. Responded to mailed test invitation	60 (72%)	9 (53%)	10 (77%)
3. Showed up for written test	53 (88%)	9 (100%)	9 (90%)
4. Passed written test	31 (58%)	4 (44%)	6 (67%)
5. Passed screening questionnaire	27 (87%)	2 (50%)	6 (100%)
6. Passed interview	9 (33%)	0 (0%)	4 (66%)
7. Passed background check	5 (55%)	N/A	2 (50%)
8. Passed medical and psych exam	5 (100%)	N/A	2 (100%)
9. Offered position	2 (40%)	N/A	2 (100%)
10. Hired	2 (100%)	N/A	2 (100%)

In the diagram above, the first column indicates the various stages in the recruitment process. The second column is divided into three parts. Each part represents one of three recruitment strategies: internet solicitation, job fairs, and the new method of extending selected invitations at colleges and universities. This new method allowed us to target recruits from minority groups by focusing on colleges and universities with minority populations. It was cost effective too, costing less than either of the other two methods. The sample size is small, but I'm confident that this method has significant potential.

From the Department to the Public

Creating a healthy environment for law enforcement requires supervisors who are committed to ethics-based policing and employ recruiting strategies that ensure a broad spectrum of qualified recruit—recruits with the appropriate personality, skill sets, and education. As a culture becomes more ethical, change becomes visible.

I've witnessed such change. I've watched residents and businesses begin to trust and work with the police after patrol officers interacted with the residents and let them know they were there to not just arrest bad actors but also to solve problems and serve. In one neighborhood, absentee landlords had allowed vacant buildings to go unsecured, attracting drug users. After residents expressed their concerns about this to beat officers, the beat officers had the city conduct building inspections and fine the owners of those buildings until they were finally secured.

In a warehouse area fronting a major traffic artery, the cut-off roadway for the trucks to stage and unload was being used by commuters as a shortcut during rush hour. That hampered truck loading and unloading. The beat officers began to periodically write tickets on vehicles violating the posted "local traffic only" signs, which eliminated the problem quickly.

Ethics-based policing gives "protect and serve" significant meaning and impact for the police and their constituents. When they work together, transformation becomes synergy.

Let's take a closer look at how to get started.

SEVEN

Training Leaders

Creating the synergy of ethics-based policing begins with training, and training begins at the top. Although the entire leadership of the department should be on board, one dedicated individual must take charge of instigating change by creating a program to train supervisors and mid-level managers for their ethical gatekeeping role.

So who is the ideal trainer? Someone who sees the need for change and is ready to take the helm. A competent, confident captain or higher-ranking police official with the ability to capture the hearts and minds of others. A man or woman with plenty of line experience who relates easily to supervisors and mid-level managers and has their implicit trust. This leader understands the concepts and goals of ethical policing, why training is critical, and the essential need for consistent support and conveyance of the message to subordinates.

After the right high-level official is identified, that person will benefit from taking classes to develop effective teaching skills, unless he or she has plenty of previous experience as an instructor. The sooner this happens, the better. Although any external program will do, such as one at a local community college, the International Association of Chiefs of Police may be a good place to begin the search for education.

When the trainer is equipped to face a class of supervisors and mid-level managers, it's time to create a program that meets the specific requirements of their department.

Big Picture Buy-In

Any program to revitalize departmental ethics must emphasize the big picture to the sergeants and mid-level managers who are key to creating and maintaining ethics-based policing. These supervisors tend to work in cloistered environments. They see only what they or their own supervisors do, and they only know what they see. They need to understand how much impact they have on their subordinates, and, in fact, how much change they can create in overall departmental operations.

Talking heads often refer to this as "buy-in." I call it "bringing those who don't know what they don't know into the fold." Renewing public trust and confidence in the police depends upon the commitment of supervisors and mid-level managers to their role as ethical gatekeepers. The entire program for developing ethics-based policing is centered around their acceptance of responsibility for holding subordinates accountable. They must understand that consistent reinforcement of good behavior and consistent consequences for unethical behavior are non-negotiable. Although "holding subordinates accountable" may carry a negative connotation, do not underplay the positive prong: recognition and rewards for subordinates who perform with high values—compelling motivators for ethical behavior.

Working as the night chief during the late 1990s, I went to the scene of a critical missing person, a seven-year-old girl who failed to show up at home after school. I was there to make sure that sufficient personnel were available for the investigation and search, and to call in more officers if necessary. The district's watch commander assured me he had plenty of officers in action. He had asked those officers for volunteers to stay beyond their tour of duty to continue the search. Every officer stayed. In fact, the whole sector of officers volunteered, and their acceptance was reported to the entire district over police radio. Several hours later, one of the officers initiated a search at the missing girl's school. They found her asleep in a cloak room.

I'm confident that rewards and recognition were the last things on these officers' minds. They were just doing the right thing. Turning the search and investigation over to the incoming shift would have caused a considerable and potentially tragic transitional delay. As those officers responded over their radios to say they were staying, the entire police district heard. When all was said and done, all those who stayed received a minor commendation. Between radioed acceptance and those commendations, a clear message was sent to all: ethical decisions are valued and rewarded.

Winning Classroom Approaches

An effective trainer will have current, thorough knowledge of departmental orders, policies, laws, and other critical written material. Part of their role is encouraging supervisors and mid-level to be experts in the books too. They must continually review the material—all of it. Supervisors can't convey the message that officers under their charge will be held accountable for ethical behavior and conduct if they don't know the laws, policies, and procedures outlining that conduct themselves.

No amount of training can compensate for a poor teacher. To create an ethical police force, your trainer will need the ability to bring mid-level supervisors on board and win their trust. I've had my greatest teaching successes not by standing in the front of the room at the lectern and talking *at* students as they feverishly took notes, but by talking *with* them. It didn't matter whether I was at a university or with subordinates in the police force. We all know what it's like to endure training classes filled with endless pontification. Not fun—unless you happen to fall asleep. The goal of ethics-based policing is too important to lose a single attendee to dreamland. Listen as much as you speak. Explain and provide examples by incorporating a little storytelling. Be willing to go back and forth with participants about the ideas you wish to share. Ask them about their experiences and invite or solicit questions.

Be ready for resistance. At least one person in attendance will probably not see any need for change, wanting things to remain as they
are. I've found success by paying particular attention to that person or
persons and engaging them in discussions. I ask for their opinions and
questions such as "What would you do?" or "How would you handle
that situation?" When possible, I offer complements like "Good question" or "Great thought." By engaging them directly, I can usually get
them to participate too.

When I address students or trainees in any setting, I acknowledge
that we all have the same goal. We're on the same team. In the case of
university students, the goal is learning the subject matter. With police,
the goal is strengthening or building an ethical police culture that will
serve everyone.

Let's say a ranking police official has stepped up and is moving with
some urgency to bring their corporals, sergeants, and lieutenants on
board by sharing a presentation and introducing them to the concept of
an ethical police force culture. I've found a three-day class with fifteen
students worked very well for me, but others may find that five days
and twenty students are optimal. Over time, class size and duration can
be fine-tuned according to feedback from attendees. Trainers should be
flexible and make changes as insight and expertise grow.

The class should be personalized and specific to the agency by incorporating discussions and examples related to departmental experience. Doing so makes it easier for the trainer to connect with the class
quickly. If attendees receive an in-depth student evaluation question-
naire at the end of each class, instructors can find out if the message
is getting through, but they will also discover ideas for improving the
class. Anonymity is fine.

I won't get into the weeds as far as lesson plans go—all the material
required is covered in part 1—but I believe the first two or three hours
on the first day are of the highest importance. In those critical first
hours, the skeptics and hard cases—in fact everyone in the class—will
decide whether ethics-based policing is going to work or not. The trainer

must capture their trust and confidence and help them understand *why* they are taking the class. The culture will not change without their full commitment to ethics, and that makes them the most valuable resource in ethics-based policing. Treat them as such.

It is important to know if students are actually learning the material presented. While the student evaluations provide good feedback about how well the trainer is doing, tests are reliable measures of student comprehension. Testing underscores the importance of the training and the critical role of ethical gatekeeping, reinforcing to the students that they must take learning seriously, whether the material is graded or marked pass/fail. It conveys the expectation that they will put what they've learned into practice. A certificate of successful training is always welcomed by those who pass the session. This, too, conveys the importance of the course and gives the student something to be proud of.

After so much effort has been made to successfully train and implement ethics-based policing, trainers should be sure to employ some form of follow-up with course graduates. A month or two after the course ends and they've had some time to apply the training to real-life operations, invite them to a round-table discussion about the course, their progress, experiences, problems, and successes. This meeting will help identify program details that may have been overlooked and improve on the program in general. It also presents an opportunity to assist anyone experiencing difficulty.

Create a Program

Let's say your department has decided to create a program establishing an ethical police culture. The high-level official chosen as the initial trainer is you. You have acquired basic teaching skills, and now you're ready to tailor a training program for your department's supervisors and mid-level managers, who will then assume responsibility for implementing a shift to the department's ethical culture.

You've read this book and understand the material well. It's time to create the program that will transform your department. You know your agency better than I do, so feel free to adapt the information that follows to best meet your needs. Emphasize areas most relevant to your department's circumstances. If your police agency has written orders, directives, or policies concerning ethical conduct, integrity, or honesty, make sure to review and incorporate them into the examples or case studies you share with your class.

To establish a solid footing for the program, spend some initial class time studying the police core virtues: prudence, trust, courage, intellectual honesty, justice, responsibility, and self-effacement of interest. If additional police core virtues would benefit your department, add them. A thorough examination of these virtues ensures that supervisors and mid-level managers understand the implications of each virtue and how they impact police work. Once the virtues are fully understood, examine how they can help create an existing ethical culture or expand an existing one. Every step along the way, stress the responsibility supervisors and mid-level managers hold for weaving police core virtues into police force culture.

Part 1 of this book includes all this information, so use it. Share the history of unethical policing and current events that have put us where we are right now. Elaborate by drawing upon familiar examples from your own department. Don't focus only on negative examples; also include examples of good ethics at work to empower and encourage your students. Emphasize the importance of keeping up to date on every rule book and every departmental procedure and policy.

Good instructor training prior to preparing your program will make planning easier and give you some ideas for how to approach your class, but here is a rough outline of a procedure that might help you get started.

1. Outline your lesson plans.

    a. Review part 1 of this book to ensure you fully understand the concepts and use examples or stories from your own agency to help students understand how they apply.

b. Divide the book concepts into sessions that feel logical for your department and the men and women you will be addressing.

c. Determine how many sessions are needed to cover the material adequately, how long each session will take, and the time span for completing the training.

d. Determine an appropriate class size.

2. Prepare your presentation and materials.

a. Develop a detailed content outline for each session of the course including relevant supporting stories or case studies. Be sure to choose stories that will intrigue your audience and take advantage of relevant situations they may have experienced. Consider questions that will inspire conversation and interactivity, such as:

 • Have you experienced this? Tell us about it.
 • Is this necessary? Why or why not?
 • What are your thoughts on this point?
 • Why do you agree or disagree with this idea?

b. Create a PowerPoint presentation to back up your main points— but don't overload the slides with text. Highlight the main ideas in the simplest form possible. Use images wherever you can.

c. Create handouts summarizing the main points of each class.

d. Develop written tests.

e. Create a student evaluation for the end of each class.

3. Establish a class schedule.

a. Provide times and dates for each session, and note the topics of discussion for each. Indicate scheduled breaks, any required dress code, and attendance requirements.

b. Highlight dates when tests are scheduled.

c. Announce the class through your department's process and appropriately notify your students and their commanders.

d. Print and distribute the schedule according to departmental protocol.

4. Review and rehearse your material.

    a. Consider your outline to be an at-a-glance guide to the class structure, *not* something to read from.

    b. Speak your material aloud. Rehearse the material you'll share until it unfolds naturally and you know it well enough to improvise.

    c. Make sure you know how to use any equipment necessary to your presentation.

5. Present the course.

    a. Use the presentation material you developed to guide each session, but be personable and flexible in your manner. Take a conversational approach. Engage with the class and encourage their participation.

    b. Be aware of the impact your presentation is having on participants and note any questions or comments they may have that could suggest improved approaches to the next session or the next time you teach the program.

    c. Ensure that each student completes an evaluation form at the end of the course. Along with the reactions you note in class, these forms will help you continue to improve the content and your teaching skills.

6. Follow up.

    a. Review the evaluation forms and your notes about the impact of each class.

    b. A month or two after the course has been completed, conduct a round-table meeting with a few participants to glean more information:

        • How has the program helped you achieve cultural change?

        • Are you discovering any areas where more training would be helpful?

        • Have you any insights that might benefit participants in future training classes?

        • Tell us about your experiences in both recognizing and

rewarding good ethical conduct and holding those accountable who fall sort?

- Have you seen a change in ethical performance of duty?
- How much, if any, resistance did you encounter?
- Has the number of citizen complaints against officer declined?
- Has there been an increase in letters from the community praising officer?
- Has there been a decrease in use of excessive force?
- Have any officers come forward and reported unethical conduct by another officer?
- Have you written any officer up for a commendation?
- Have you written any officer up for disciplinary action?

6. Fine-tune your presentation.
   a. Based on the evaluation forms and information gleaned from your meeting with program participants, review and adjust your presentation.
   b. Include any changes you noted yourself—for example, improvements to your PowerPoint presentation or handouts.

Congratulations! Now that you have trained your first group of supervisors and first-line managers, it's up to them to carry the baton and convey expectations that will transform your department's culture. Make sure they know that you will always be there to support them.

Extend the Culture, Share the Program

Once your program is up and running effectively, consider how to extend its reach. After all, the objective of training is not only to create an ethical culture but to perpetuate that culture. In large departments, one ranking police official as a trainer will not be enough. Others will have to step up. Each new group of trainers should work with the first trainer to acquire comparable skills. The trainer can share the original program and support materials with them. Pointers drawn from experience will help too, such as questions received from students and how they responded. Perhaps most importantly, the experienced trainer may have suggestions for bringing supervisors and mid-level managers on board—not because they're ordered to, but because they *want* to, because they understand the value of ethics-based policing objectives.

Smaller departments can share their knowledge with other agencies. One expert might train leaders in a number of towns, municipalities, sheriffs' departments, townships, and small city police forces. Eventually, all existing first-line supervisors and mid-level managers in a given geographical area will be trained.

Perpetuate the Culture

By ensuring everyone within a police department is fully trained in ethics-based policing, an ethical culture will take root. It will spread. Officers promoted to sergeant or lieutenant receive ethical culture training alongside leadership training. In departments offering periodic in-service training for veteran officers, ethical training is included. In the academy, new recruits are primed on police core virtues and their implications. Of course, each of these groups—leaders, veteran officers, and rookies—require training nuanced to meet their needs. As trainers become more experienced, they can adapt their programs accordingly. And of course, supervisors and mid-level managers will reinforce the lessons of ethical policing by holding officers accountable for their behavior.

In my assignment as captain in the Special Operations Division (SOD), I saw the power of an ethical culture firsthand. The SOD was comprised of veteran officers who had applied for their roles and went through a rigorous selection process. These highly trained officers were the first ones called to handle major demonstrations, civil disobedience, unruly crowds, and riots, many of which were violent in nature.

Though I attended many such situations while I was at SOD, I never witnessed nor heard of a SOD officer losing composure or using excessive force or profanity. They were professional, skilled, and courageous. They understood and believed in ethics-based policing. Even though they were tested time and time again in the most trying circumstances, they never failed to display dedication and commitment to the ethical policing.

This ethical culture was not a hindrance. It did not tie their hands, and it did not expose them to more danger. They were confident and competent, and I might add, proud, to work in that environment. They did not fear being videoed by the media or public because they knew what to do and they knew what not to do. Their conduct and performance of duty were based on police core virtues.

Think what a department would be like if all its members were like this! It is not impossible, but it takes continual effort. That effort should extend not only to sworn members of the department but also to civilian personnel, particularly those who work closely with officers, such as communication dispatchers or police vehicle maintenance technicians. Contributions, suggestions, and recommendations should be considered from all.

Certain hours of the day and days of the week are naturally slower. Take advantage of these times to perpetuate an ethical culture. For example, officers on patrol are always listening to the police radio. When there are fewer calls for service, significant dead air can be put to use by an alert dispatcher who broadcasts radio quips, or brief messages, about ethics and operations to all units. A new quip can be shared by the dispatcher once or twice every tour of duty.

In some communities, fear of crime can be a significant issue. It affects the quality of life for residents, and some people limit their interactions with others because they are afraid to venture outside their homes, especially when it's dark and the streets are empty. A police presence reduces fear and increases resident comfort level, but their presence won't help if they aren't clearly visible.

In Washington, DC, vehicle maintenance technicians determined how to make marked cars more visible after dark. By switching some wires so that two blue lights stayed illuminated at all times, residents could easily spot a marked vehicle patrolling the neighborhood.

Ethical culture nurtures public trust. Individuals and communities know the police will protect and serve them, and in turn, they will be more supportive of law enforcement.

EIGHT

Conveying Expectations

I t is critical that culture-setting corporals, sergeants, and lieutenants agree to tackle messaging as a team—and take a consistent, unambiguous approach to sharing it. Their expectations for ethical behavior should extend to all aspects of police work. Any lack of consistency or clarity is dangerous. It leads to confusion and misunderstanding about expectations at every level—from operations and management to duty and execution of service.

A week of extended roll calls, an early reporting time, or a holdover from a tour or tours of duty should provide the uninterrupted time necessary to introduce officers to ethics-based policing. Expectations must be conveyed at every opportunity and incorporate departmental experience. Subordinates understanding, buy-in, and adoption of this new approach can be significantly enhanced and improved if the department's current state of affairs and previous experiences are braided into the presentation.

Reinforcing Direction

Once officers have been introduced to the principles of ethics-based policing, reinforcing them on a continual basis will preempt confusion, prevent mediocrity, and eliminate unethical behavior. This consistency lets officers know that rewards and recognition will go to those who deserve it. They'll understand how any unethical behavior can fuel public loss of trust and even downright hostility, and they should know that their supervisors will hold them accountable for behavior, good or bad.

Ethical failure appears in all areas of the job:

- Neglecting to complete a follow-up police report
- Conducting an inadequate preliminary investigation, which means performing a hasty check for witnesses, evidence, and property that brings inadequate results
- Showing up late for a detailed assignment
- Failing to be in possession of credentials at inspections
- Neglecting to record critical information in notebooks during roll call
- Leaving the patrol car with little fuel for officers on the next tour of duty

All these and any number of other minor violations cannot go unchallenged or ignored. Although every ethical failure may not involve formal administrative disciplinary action, calling out offenders on their behavior sends a strong message.

As important as it is to hold officers accountable for minor violations, it is equally important to hold them responsible for expected, but nonetheless, good work. For example, an officer responds to an armed robbery that has just taken place. The officer quickly obtains a detailed description of the suspect, his method and direction of flight, and the elapsed time since the incident. This attention to protocol results in the apprehension of the suspect. A supervisor intent on holding all officers accountable singles out the officer's actions as an example of how a general radio broadcast should be done.

Police organization leadership should expect and foster superior performance from those under their charge. The chief of police can't be the only one conveying high expectations. Standards must be communicated by everyone in the chain of command. First-line supervisors and mid-level managers must continually ensure that high expectations are communicated and understood by the police officers in their units, and they need support.

In chapter 2, I discussed how a new leader took steps to improve the function and morale of a bomber unit in the movie *Twelve O'clock High*. Communicating high expectations and demanding their enforcement was key to his transformation strategy. Clearly defined and communicated expectations set vital guideposts for police officers too. If these expectations are framed around police core virtues, a positive, high-functioning police culture can be developed and maintained.

Conveying expectations involves more than occasionally talking about them at roll call. It requires continuous reinforcement during roll call, through casual encounters, and over exchanges with subordinates as a group or as individuals. Subordinates must be held accountable for any failure to perform duties ethically, sending a clear message about expectations to all officers. Rewarding and recognizing those who perform their sworn duty in an ethical manner also sends a clear message. When guideposts are established, an ethical culture is born or strengthened.

The expectations promoted through supervision and leadership mirror the Pygmalion effect. In the play *Pygmalion*, by George Bernard Shaw, a cockney flower girl is changed through the efforts of Professor Higgins who polishes the flower girl's appearance and attitude to make her a lady. His expectation of her potential to become a lady changes her behavior.

So what does this metaphor have to do with police operations? J. Sterling Livingston linked the Pygmalion effect to management in this way: "What managers expect of their subordinates and how they treat them largely determine their performance and progress."[1] The Pygmalion effect is a well-acknowledged psychological phenomenon: high expectations lead to improved performance in a given area. It occurs in the workplace when managers raise their expectations for the behavior of workers, which spurs an increase in worker performance.

A single exposure to a new expectation is not enough. How often expectations must be conveyed depends upon the amount of change required, the seriousness of the problem being addressed, and the level of resistance encountered. In some agencies, a major paradigm shift is in order. Regardless, resistance to new expectations can be anticipated from at least some officers and also from the public, particularly if they've lost trust in law enforcement. Public trust and confidence can be difficult to recapture, especially from the disenfranchised, but persistent ethical performance from the police will eventually change public opinion and garner support from many. Steeling officers to face angst and uneasiness among their peers and resistance from the public requires continuous, consistent, and often daily messaging from supervisors. It will be challenging and perhaps difficult, but it must be done with urgency and serious commitment, consistency, and energy.

During the late 1980s while I was with the DC police, a change was initiated in police radio communication protocols. When officers were given radio assignments from the police dispatcher, they were now to advise the dispatcher when they were on the scene or at the location of the call. This simple change took over six months to institute or fold into standard operating procedure.

A much more significant change like transforming departmental culture won't happen overnight. Patience, determination, and consistent reinforcement of expectations are required. No effort should be spared. Failure to establish and reinforce directions for officers in the performance of their sworn duty will result in mediocre police service. We've seen the results of mediocre or poor police service, and it is unacceptable. To effectively serve the public, highly motivated officers are essential, and the heavy responsibility for motivating them rests with corporals, sergeants, and lieutenants.

Conducting Effective Roll Calls

Roll call is perhaps the most valuable tour of duty segment for supervisors focused on ethical policing. Prior to each shift, patrol officers gather at one location to be read dispatches and receive their assignments for that day. They are brought up to speed with any developments and information relevant to their duties, and at the end of roll call, they are inspected for appearance and proper equipment.

Much can be accomplished in this face-to-face group meeting. Roll call provides an opportunity to publicly call out officers who clearly performed their duties with the core virtues in mind. From time to time, citizens write letters to the department complementing or praising an officer's service to them. Supervisors can read these letters at roll call so everyone can see the results of good police work. When sergeants and lieutenants write up subordinates for commendations to officially recognize superior performance of duty, these commendations should be read at roll calls or posted on a bulletin board.

Recognition, especially public recognition, is a powerful motivator, one I took every opportunity to employ. In the mid-1990s, I captained a patrol sector in Washington, DC. On one particularly bitter fall evening, shortly after eleven o'clock, most marked patrol cars were heading back to the station where they would await the dispatched call to turn over their assigned scout car to their relief, at the end of their tour of duty. Before relief was announced, a 911 call reported a woman screaming in a wooded area abutting a major city road. The police radio dispatcher assigned two marked patrol calls to investigate.

Since it was my personal responsibility to make sure all those under my charge were in safe or accounted for before I checked off, I headed to the scene to provide some oversight and closure for the shift. I always responded to "HOT" or urgent emergency calls and priority assignments. They often were of significant importance. When necessary, I took control of the scene and all responsibility. The two units assigned to the call expedited their arrival with lights and siren. By the time I arrived about ten minutes later, they had cleared the call as "nothing found" and were on their way back to the station. Later that evening, I heard a different side of the story unfold over the radio. An officer called for backup in that area and requested a transport vehicle.

As it turned out, the first unit to arrive on the scene had rolled down their windows, turned on their spotlights, and slowly drove along the road searching for sounds of disruption. Finding none, they drove away.

As they exited the area, another marked car pulled up with a single officer inside. Although the call was on that officer's assigned patrol beat, he had not received the assignment because he was patrolling alone, and standard operating procedure stipulated assigning two officer units to dangerous calls.

Taking personal responsibility for the area, the lone officer informed the dispatcher that he wanted to be held momentarily at that location. He slid into his raincoat. With flashlight in hand, he entered the wet and muddy wooded area. A muffled scream arose not twenty yards off the road. He sprinted toward the sound and found a man hovered over a partially clothed woman and covering her face with his hands. Holding his gun, the officer ordered the man off the woman. He had the man lay face down on the ground with his fingers locked behind his head. Then the officer called for backup. When help arrived, the officer made the arrest for assault with intent to rape.

Instead of taking a quick drive past the area where the incident occurred, this officer took the time to investigate. His effort prevented a rape and possibly saved a life. It was an example of not only great cop work but police work that demonstrated core values. The citizen who made the 911 call about a woman screaming for help *trusted* police to come quickly. He or she trusted that responding officers would search for someone who may have been in danger and take action if necessary. The lone arresting officer showed *courage* to venture into the dark wooded area alone, persevering against the discomfort of miserable weather conditions and potential danger. He exhibited both mental and moral strength and *self-effacement of interests* by placing the woman in danger before his own well-being.

The incident took place as he neared his check off time—just like the two officers who had arrived before him. Whether he found anything or not, he knew he would leave the job late. Still, he put duty ahead of getting off work on time. He was aware of his obligations as a police officer to serve and protect, and knew that his superiors would hold him *accountable* for his actions. The ethical culture we were promoting had taken root in his head and his heart.

Now the roll call tool comes into play. The next day, I singled out the arresting officer during roll call, shared the story of the arrest with emphasis on his exceptional police work, and outlined its relationship to the core virtues. I wrote him up for a commendation, which was presented to him several weeks later—again during roll call. He received a standing ovation.

Note that in both of these roll call instances, not a word was spoken about or to the officers who took the initial call and cleared the assignment with "nothing found." I didn't need to say anything. Red faces and an inability to look me in the eye told me they were humiliated and embarrassed. Without directly implicating them in any way, an important message was sent and received. Everyone in the unit heard the complete story through the grapevine, and everyone in the unit learned the lesson too: ethical behavior is expected and rewarded.

Unfortunately, the thirty-minute golden opportunity of roll call is often rushed. There's almost an unwritten rule to hurry through roll call to relieve on-duty officers and send the next shift out. While this is understandable, dedicating ten or fifteen minutes to emphasize core values a few times a week is worth far more than the time invested. Reinforcing desired behavior prevents ethical lapses and institutes an ethical culture faster, which in turn hastens a public return to trust.

At each roll call, the supervisor can take a few moments to review their department's directives on ethical conduct and discuss one of the core virtues or examples of ethical police work. It's not a Band-Aid or a quick fix, but rather, a strategy for building and maintaining ethics-based policing throughout police officers' careers.

At the conclusion of roll call, the supervisor should conduct a visual inspection to ensure all unit members are appropriately dressed and equipped for their roles. This is just another step to take responsibility for subordinates and hold them accountable for every aspect of the job. After attending thousands of inspections, I've seen all kinds of things that don't pass muster, from empty holsters and sockless feet to missing driver's licenses and badges, intoxication, disallowed body piercings, and green hair. These kinds of oversights threaten public trust. Roll call is the perfect time to convey department expectations to the unit—expectations of not only ethical conduct, but also the operational performance of doing police work.

During my career, I had the opportunity to work with many, many fine officers. These high-performing standouts always conducted themselves ethically. I spent most of my career in lower socio-economic neighborhoods where the calls for service were high, especially on Friday and Saturday evenings. It was not unusual for a marked patrol unit to handle over twenty-five radio assignments during one tour of duty. At times, assignments were stacked—put on hold—by the dispatcher because every marked unit was already on an assignment. At such times, even sergeants answered service calls. As each unit cleared an assignment, they would wait for the dispatcher to give them another.

One standout officer understood how busy the calls for service were during these hectic times. When he cleared a call, he did not wait for the dispatcher to call him. He'd jump right in and ask what was next. Occasionally, the next assignment was off his patrol beat. He didn't care. "No problem, I can take it," he'd say. Sometimes the next assignment mandated a two-officer response. "Let me take it anyway," he would say to the dispatcher. "I'll check it out and keep you advised."

I took every opportunity to compliment and encourage this officer personally and also publicly for his operational performance. As an informal leader, he was doing yeoman's work. And, of course, his performance evaluations were always outstanding. Eventually, other officers caught on to the praise this lone officer received for his effort. His conduct became contagious, habit forming, and, eventually, expected. Even when he was not on duty, other officers began querying the dispatcher for any pending assignments.

This example highlights the idea that this officer responded to expectations for a high level of operational performance. As I said before, ethical and operational performance of duty run parallel and often intersect; an action is both ethical and operational in nature at the same time. *Trust* is an ethical virtue. This officer understood that the public had placed their trust in him to protect and serve them. He knew they were relying on his character and ability. Operationally, at busy times such as these, volunteering for assignments made him stand out. So here the parallels intersect, a high volume of calls for service showed in his ethical values, trust, and high operational performance by taking on calls that were outside of his response area. This officer's conduct contributed to high morale, esprit de corps, commitment and dedication in the unit, and the best service to the public that could be rendered. Imagine a department full of officers like him!

Open mic days proved to be a useful tool during roll call. It gave officers an opportunity to speak their mind. I generally scheduled it on Fridays when manpower was high because calls for service were high. Only the officers and their sergeants were in the room, and the senior sergeant ran the session. Open Mic Friday opened the door for any officer to bring up any concerns, questions, or grievances. It provided opportunities to talk about big-picture questions, build trust, and explain orders or directions. Supervisors wove core virtues into the discussion, always working on the ethical culture.

For instance, through attending community meetings, I had discovered that many residents were unhappy because they never saw the police in their area. It made them uneasy and contributed to a fear of crime, regardless of the actual level of crime in their neighborhood. I understood that the fear of crime diminished their quality of life. In response, I had ordered my sergeants and lieutenants to have scout car officers park in these areas for ten minutes, three times during each tour of duty, and get out and walk the streets.

Although I explained my reasoning for this initiative to supervisors, that reasoning didn't make it to all the officers. The officers raised questions about the initiative on Open Mic Friday. The attending senior sergeant explained that their short walks and parked, marked car increased police visibility in the area. That visibility made residents feel they were being served and protected, decreasing their fear of crime. Quality of life improved as citizens felt safer and freer to move about. Public trust is essential. Once the reasoning for the walks was made clear, officers complied.

In summary an effective roll call encompasses four steps:

1. Takes every opportunity to recognize superior ethical and operational duty in roll calls.
2. Makes time for candid discussions, feedback, questions, and issues during roll calls.
3. Conveys expectations and sets the tone of professional appearance with daily inspections.
4. Takes a few moments to go over departmental ethical and operational directives.

Other Messaging Opportunities

Expectations can be delivered loud and clear or delivered subtly. They can be written or shared face-to-face. For serious problems and issues, it is necessary to utilize every approach and every opportunity. Don't overlook the powerful tool of recognizing officers who exhibit conduct in accordance to communicated expectations. Use whatever means at your disposal, including roll call, to reinforce good behavior. For example, if the public you serve has clearly exhibited deteriorated trust and confidence toward the police, make sure you share any messages or letters of appreciation from community members during roll call. Place letters on a bulletin board. As the power of positive community feedback for an officer increases, so should the recognition and reward. Consideration should be given to commendations, a higher performance evaluation, more responsibility, more flexibility.

Building public trust and confidence is a good thing not only for officers involved, but also for their fellow officers—some of whom may not have taken your messages about expectations seriously. Clearly, conveying expectations is a powerful force. It can go a long way in building integrity in a police department and, importantly, building public support, confidence, and trust through high-caliber police service.

As obvious and important as clear communication may be, it doesn't always happen, particularly when it comes to expectations of high performance. I witnessed the effect of such failure firsthand when I was with the Washington, DC, Metropolitan Police Department. Two support units were available for proactive patrol under my command in a drug-plagued, crime-ridden area. One group, Motor Tact, consisted of ten motorcycle officers with a reputation for average performance at best. The other unit, Power Shift, consisted of fifteen officers who worked casual clothes or in uniform, in marked or unmarked cars, depending on what I tasked them with. Both units worked the same areas during the same tours of duty.

Power Shift had been together for some time. My expectations for high performance had been conveyed to them frequently, and those expectations were continually reinforced. Week after week, they displayed superior ethics in the execution of their duties—from gun seizures and felony arrests to recovering large quantities of drugs. Motor Tact, on the other hand, wrote tickets, handled special details, and made few arrests. I assumed that was all they could do. Looking back, I see that I failed to convey my high-performance expectations to Motor Tact as I had with Power Shift.

During the summer of 1995, the whole Power Shift unit was detailed out to assist with a major drug investigation. The assignment would keep them off my roster for at least four months, leaving me with what I believed to be one feeble unit: Motor Tact. In Power Shift's absence, Motor Tact would be required to work in a high crime area and attack Part 1 offenses, such as murder, rape, robbery, aggravated assault, burglary, larceny, stolen vehicle, and arson.

Without other highly trained units at my disposal, I began to convey the same expectations to Motor Tact that I had been conveying to Power Shift. I met with the Motor Tact officers in my office, wanting our meeting to be informal, open, comfortable, and relaxed. When all were present, I spoke:

"The Power Shift is going to be gone for some months, but their absence does not mean the important work of protecting residents and serious crime fighting can be put on hold. Those we swore to protect need your help, and I need your help. I need you to step up and step into the work that Power Shift had been doing. You know you all can do this. I know you can. I am at your side. Anything you need from me you just ask." Different players, same objective.

I conveyed in detail the tactics and strategies I wanted them to employ, but my goal was to inspire them. I wanted them to step up not just because I was *directing* them to, but because they *wanted* to. After working together for over a year, we shared mutual trust. They knew I offered no sticks, only carrots: reward, recognition, and higher status. To my surprise and relief, they were eager and excited by the assignment. I was embarrassed to realize that I had previously failed to convey high expectations by providing detailed guidance and direction.

The change in Motor Tact's performance was almost immediate. Within one week, their behavior and attitude shifted, approaching that of the Power Shift. Clearly, the Motor Tact unit was capable of performing at whatever level was expected of them—as long as the expectation was conveyed. That served as an important lesson for me. I had failed Motor Tact, but I had also failed the citizens of my district. Residents didn't need traffic enforcement; they needed bad actors removed from the area.

The link between expectations and performance is evident far beyond police agencies. The late Jaime Escalante, a former teacher in Los Angeles, believed that his inner-city high school students were as capable of learning as students in any other high school. He was convinced they could learn calculus. When Escalante communicated his expectation to students and offered the assistance they needed, they did indeed learn calculus and continued on to other successes.[2]

The public has granted awesome power and authority to the police. In return, the public has the right to expect police to conduct themselves ethically and to perform at a high level. To achieve ethical, high-level performance, officers must know what is expected of them, what the limits and rules are, and what consequences await them for behaving as they should and as they shouldn't. When expectations are uncertain, limits are shifting, or rules are arbitrarily enforced, behavior is inconsistent. A superior's expectations must be clearly established, communicated, understood, and enforced. Conveying expectations can guide a departments ethical conduct as well as its performance, as described earlier in my experience with the Motor Tact unit. They were always ethically grounded in their duty, but when I provided some direction and told them what I expected, their performance took a major jump.

Communication of expectations gives direction. When some departments suffer from a loss of public confidence and trust or are in the middle of organizational change, officers may be left shaking their heads. They may question why they should go out and risk their lives, serve, protect, and keep the peace for a belligerent public. Like me, they took the Uniformed Services Oath of Office, swearing to uphold the Constitution and to protect and serve. There was no caveat in the oath suggesting that it applied to only those who liked the police.

Without clear direction, officers facing uncertain support from the public may deliver mediocre police service at best. Especially now, when frustration with policing is so high across the country, expectations must be clearly conveyed and enacted to stop fanning flames of apprehension and outright animosity. Why would officers reach out to a frustrated community or take steps to build public trust and confidence if they aren't directly told to do so—and told how to go about it? Why would an officer search for underlying conditions behind the loss of public trust and confidence if that expectation hadn't been conveyed?

Although much work needs to be done, I believe that dedicated, committed, resourceful, ethical men and women in the ranks of corporal, sergeant, and lieutenant are up to the task.

Track Your Progress

To establish ethics-based policing, I recommend departments document every effort made from the very first day. You know the drill: date, time, location, who, what, when, and how. When things turn around, someone is sure to say that the police had nothing to do with it. It changed because of whatever measure an outside agency or government put in place. Politicians, bureaucrats, or social scientists will claim credit under the false assumption that what they said or did changed things. Because they changed things, they are now experts on policing.

For example, a report on an ethical training class would include the rank, qualifications, and experience of each person who attended and provide an attendance summary. It would include the dates of each class, summarize the themes or content of those classes, list the tests or exams given and scores received, and list class ratings drawn from student evaluation forms. These are called process measures—or evidence of your efforts—will clearly illustrate the impact that the implementation of ethics-based policing had on your department and how well expectations were conveyed.

NINE

Mentoring First-Line Supervisors

From time to time, officers will be promoted to the role of sergeant, assuming responsibility for supervising subordinates and holding them accountable. Even if they previously served as an officer in an ethics-based department, additional training and support will ensure they have the necessary skills and abilities required to perpetuate the ethical culture in their new roll.

New Sergeants

If new sergeants are fortunate, they may have an opportunity to attend a first-line supervisor's class or school for a few weeks. A good program will teach them a host of useful techniques, tactics, and strategies to enhance their ability to lead and motivate their charges. Many skills are essential for leadership, such as operations management, critical thinking, decision-making, people skills, communication skills like public speaking, and more. But formal classes aren't always available. Sometimes new sergeants find themselves in charge of a squad of police officers with little support.

Newcomers have a lot to learn and experience. If police departments want to ensure they succeed, leadership has a responsibility to assist and counsel them. Most departments have field-training officers to coach and mentor rookies. This is regarded as a worthwhile and expected practice for developing effective police officers. The same consideration should be given to newly promoted sergeants. With an established, competent lieutenant or captain to coach and mentor them, new supervisors demonstrate vastly improved performance. As discussed in part 1 at length, first-line supervisors are the backbone of any department. Their skills are critical to strengthening or building an ethical culture. Every possible approach to ensuring their success must be considered.

New sergeants may or may not have been exposed to an ethical culture during their service as an officer. Regardless, there is a difference between assuming responsibility for one's own behavior and holding an entire squad of officers accountable. New sergeants must be convinced that their leadership is essential to an ethical culture. They must understand that it is their responsibility to hold officers accountable, and they must be shown how to do so. Most supervisors and managers learn by experience. They are more likely to learn relevant leadership skills and values if they are exposed to a variety of developmental experiences on the job and receive appropriate coaching and mentoring from superiors who model police core values and skills for enforcing an ethical culture. This kind of development should be a major focus of upper-level management in any police department.

During difficult job transitions, such as a new promotion to leadership or a transfer to another unit, mentors facilitate adjustment, learning, and stress reduction. Research shows that mentoring provides two functions for the mentee. The first, a psycho-social function, includes acceptance and encouragement. The second, a counseling and career-facilitation function, includes sponsorship, protection from less-than-enlightened superiors, support for managing challenging assignments, and the exposure and visibility required to establish a firm leadership role. It can take time for mentees to step out of their pre-promotion role and step up to their new supervisory position. Studies show that mentoring results in more career advancement and success for the mentee.

The benefits of mentoring aren't limited to the individual being mentored. Mentors also benefit from the experience because it is likely to increase their job satisfaction. As they teach others, their own leadership skills grow. The focus on building an ethical culture becomes even more deeply ingrained. Mentoring given and mentoring received both predicted career success. According to the acclaimed author, speaker, and organizational consultant Mary Abbajay,

> The benefits of mentoring are myriad. For individuals, studies show that good mentoring can lead to greater career success, including promotions, raises, and increased opportunities. Organizations that embrace mentoring are rewarded with higher levels of employee engagement, retention and knowledge sharing. In fact, mentoring has proved so beneficial that 71 percent of Fortune 500 companies offer mentoring programs to their employees.[1]

Coaching and mentoring can provide a variety of potential benefits. They foster mutually cooperative relationships between the coach/mentor—usually a captain or lieutenant—and the new sergeant. The captain or lieutenant facilitates the sergeant's career advancement, and the sergeant reciprocates by being helpful, cooperative, and loyal to the captain or lieutenant. Coaching and mentoring help identify promising subordinate officials and prepare them to fill positions of greater responsibility. That can increase subordinate job satisfaction and commitment to the police organization. Mentors experience the intrinsic reward of helping others grow and develop. All of this is good for the ethical culture.

Mentorship Approaches

The following nine approaches can provide solid coaching and mentorship to new leaders.

1. Provide Role Models

Observing the interpersonal and professional behavior of competent, effective, and experienced leaders has a dramatic impact on police culture. Essentially, leaders, as role models, pass their behavior on. As new sergeants model the effective performance they observe in their superiors, their own behaviors are molded and strengthened, and they become role models for their subordinates.

Setting a worthy example is a powerful tool for building or maintaining an ethical police culture. As a rookie sergeant, I was fortunate to have the mentorship of a skilled and knowledgeable captain. His friendly demeanor made it easy for me to emulate him. I paid attention to his bearing, comportment, and conduct and witnessed his ethical values, all of which influenced me significantly. To this day, I credit him for his considerable contribution to my success.

2. Identify Needs

One of the first steps toward developing new supervisors' skills is to determine what they already know about police core virtues and establishing or maintaining ethics-based policing. Look for any discrepancies between current skills and required skills. Pay attention to any questions the mentee might ask. Those questions will clearly reveal gaps in knowledge. The mentor can then respond to fill those gaps, emphasizing values and reinforcing them among subordinates.

Promotion and assignment to a patrol unit can be major change for any new sergeant, but it can be harder for some than others, especially in larger departments with a wide range of specialized duties. A long-time detective who is promoted to sergeant will soon discover that supervising a patrol squad and building an ethical culture is quite different from working an investigative unit. Conducting inspections, handling major traffic accidents, leading missing person investigations, conducting community meetings, and a litany of other basic supervisory patrol functions will be new. It's up to experienced supervisors to identify the gaps.

If sergeants in training understand the big-picture reasons for the expectations placed upon them, they are more likely to participate. It may be helpful to relate training content to the individual's needs, interests, and career ambitions. Describe learning objectives in terms of specific knowledge or behaviors that relate to job requirements rather than vague personality abilities or traits. For instance, rather than telling sergeants they need to show confidence, tell them that they need to know the departments orders, policies, and procedures because their subordinates see them as a subject matter expert on the books. With this knowledge, they will be competent, leading to confidence.

Set learning objectives to improve their competency. Learning the police core virtues establishes a foundation for instilling or upholding an ethical culture. Knowing departmental directives enhances their operational skills. And, of course, foundational to all of this, is taking responsibility. It's the key to their success, and it's expected by the public, subordinates, peers, and superiors.

3. Facilitate Learning

Mentors must ensure that the sergeants and first-line supervisors they relate to are well-versed in the concepts, terms, rules, and procedures of the department, and understand them. They must be well versed in core virtues and knowledgeable about operations before they can demand accountability from their subordinates. To investigate an accusation of use of excessive force, for example, the department may have just four outcomes for complaint resolution: sustained, not sustained, exonerated, or unfounded. The sergeant in charge must have a firm grasp on what each term means and when and how they apply, based on the investigation.

Because there is so much to learn, ease new sergeants into their roles with cut and dry cases. For example, one of their duties may include handling the scene and paperwork for a scout car accident. Introduce them to procedures through an accident with minor damage and no injuries that was clearly the fault of the other driver. That is far less complicated than an accident where the scout car needs towing, two officers and a civilian sustained injury, and conflicting statements and evidence arise. As new sergeants successfully complete basic tasks, they will become more confident and capable of performing more complex ones.

A new detective's first case is never a homicide. Similarly, high-profile, complicated cases shouldn't be assigned to a brand-new supervisor. If, say, an officer is accused of using excessive force that results in a serious injury, and the accusation is supported by a clear and convincing video, an in-depth investigation and serious administrative disciplinary action are likely. Such an investigation should be conducted by an experienced, skilled supervisor with the new supervisor as copilot.

Utilize the existing skills of a newly promoted patrol sergeant. He may have testified many times in grand juries or trials, so he has some skill in addressing groups of people. The coach can build on that skill. Perhaps the coach learns that during the previous tour of duty, one of the new supervisor's subordinates demonstrated ethical behavior that was clearly grounded in the police core virtues. The coach could encourage the new sergeant to recognize that officer publicly during the next roll call.

4. Practice with Feedback

It may be helpful to have new sergeants practice procedures or tasks and then critique their responses. Explain why something was done incorrectly or suggest improvements and help the sergeant understand how to do better. Mistakes should be viewed as learning experiences, not personal failures.

Sergeants may be expected to conduct inspections following roll call before their officers take their assignments. While a new sergeant may have been inspected many times during roll call, conducting an inspection will be new. They may walk down the line of officers and miss deficiencies or notice but fail to address them. Perhaps an officer has only one extra pistol magazine in their pouch instead of the required two. Another officer may wear a shirt so wrinkled that it looks like he slept in it. If the new sergeant doesn't respond to such oversights, bring attention to them for improvement and competency.

5. Encourage Skill Application

Encourage new sergeants continually, and at times push them into applying their skills. It may be uncomfortable, but with practice comes more confidence and increased performance. I have seen salty and cynical officers test rookie sergeants during roll call to take measure of their sand and grit by complaining or questioning them inappropriately. In one such instance, the new sergeant responded, "This is neither the time nor the place to bring that up, but I will be more than happy to discuss this or answer your questions in my office following the conclusion of inspection." The new sergeant maintained his composure and control and, at the same time, sent a message: he was the supervisor. He was confident and competent.

6. Show Concern

A basic principle of mentoring is to express genuine concern for the personal development and career progress of subordinates. This goes hand in hand with establishing ethics-based policing and fostering committed, dedicated, and responsible personnel. With this kind of care, it is easier and more natural for new sergeants to learn and grow in the performance of duty and model such behaviors for their subordinates. I referred earlier to the captain who mentored me early in my career. Not only did he model exemplary performance of duty, but he always encouraged me to strive for high achievement and future promotion. He was positive and encouraging about my day-to-day performance as well as about my future with the department.

7. Verify Success

For coaches to verify that new sergeants have successfully learned targeted skills and knowledge, they might attend roll calls run by the new sergeants or perhaps sign off on a proposed disciplinary action generated by them. This might include approving a commendation for ethical performance of duty written by the new sergeants or simply telling them they did a good job handling a particular event or situation.

8. Offer Recognition and Praise

Recognition and praise are important. They reinforce a job well done and can lead to repetition of that same behavior. New supervisors need such reinforcement as much as the officers they lead. A coach's praise helps forge a trusting relationship with the sergeant.

As a rookie sergeant, I found myself in a vehicle pursuit of a homicide suspect after he had circumvented a roadblock. It was just me and the suspect, and the chase lasted no more than ten minutes. The dispatcher cleared the radio air for me, so I was the only one talking, giving my direction of travel several times a minute. The entire police district I was assigned to could hear. The suspect crashed and bailed out of his vehicle, resulting in foot pursuit. I caught and held him until reinforcements arrived.

The captain, my mentor, also showed up on the scene. He told me privately that my broadcasts had been the coolest, calmest, and most professional he had ever heard. What a boost! The whole police district I was assigned to had been listening to my radio transmissions, and he had those words for me. That was a confidence builder. Especially since it had been years since I had been involved in an emergency pursuit.

9. Provide Ample Time

Coaching isn't completed in days or weeks. It's an ongoing process. Priorities should be identified and tackled. As new supervisors become more confident and competent, mentors will loosen the reins and eventually release them. But the relationship doesn't come to an end. New supervisors know they will always have someone to turn to for guidance on particularly difficult issues. Obviously, building an ethical culture and how to maintain one would be at the top of the list and an ongoing project.

TEN

Credible and Consistent Leadership

Corporals, sergeants, and lieutenants must be credible. They must be clear. They must consistently take the responsibility of holding their subordinates accountable for all behavior, good and bad. They must not allow ethical lines to be crossed, or those lines will become blurred, eroding supervisor credibility.

Ethics and the expectation for a high level of performance must extend to every single action officers take. If they never use excessive force or demeaning language and they are honest and follow all the other police core virtues, but they display mediocre effort in their performance of operational duty, they must be held accountable for lack of effort.

For example, consider a busy Saturday evening tour of duty. Radio assignments are stacked waiting for available units to clear one assignment so they can be dispatched to another. An officer completes a traffic accident report, but thirty minutes pass before he advises the dispatcher he's clear for another assignment. While thirty minutes of unaccounted time is clearly an operational issue to address, it also has ethical connotations regarding responsibility and duty. That officer failed to meet his obligations on several levels—his obligation to the citizens who require his service, to the peers who must pick up the slack, to the department whose reputation is on the line, and to the profession of policing itself. It only takes one rotten apple to spoil the barrel.

Left unchallenged, that operational act blurs the ethical line of responsibility. If the supervisor doesn't hold that officer accountable for operational irresponsibility, the supervisor's credibility and ethics can be questioned. If the sergeant initiates disciplinary action that requires approval from the chain of command, each link within that command has a duty to seriously consider the recommendation. Otherwise, the ethical culture falters.

Early in my career as a detective, a friend who was a uniform patrol officer met me for breakfast at 9:15 one weekday morning. The waitress just delivered our meals when a sergeant walked in. He looked at the uniform officer and said, "You know better than that."

My uniformed friend got up, left his breakfast, and walked out, followed by the sergeant. With a few short words, the sergeant reminded his charge that uniformed patrol officers were prohibited from going out of service to eat during morning or evening rush hour. The morning rush hour wasn't over until 9:30 am. My friend, the patrol officer, was challenged and held accountable. This is a simple but effective example.

Subject Matter Experts

Subordinate officers view superior officers as subject matter experts, as well they should. That means effective, ethical superiors must consistently study their department's policies, procedures, and general orders, as well as the police manual, the criminal code, traffic regulations, the municipal code, laws of search and seizure, and a plethora of other information subject to regular updates. They must be well-versed in rules, regulations, and all the ins and outs of ethical police conduct. Their roles involve more than classifying crimes or determining the elements of a crime or identifying probable cause misdemeanors. Superiors must continually perform police service at a high level. It means showing initiative and effort. It means attending to any "slackers," such as the officer who took an unscheduled thirty-minute break before contacting dispatch for another assignment.

Citizens have legitimate expectations that officers know what they are doing, and that what they are doing is lawful and in accordance with department orders, policies, and procedures. A police squad, section, or platoon expects their superior to know what they are doing and turns to them for guidance and direction. For answers. The public has expectations of the officers, and the officers have expectations of their superiors. How can superiors hold their subordinates responsible and accountable if they do not live by these principles themselves?

Whether on the scene of a domestic incident involving an off-duty officer, a critical missing persons incident involving a five-year-old, a barricaded and armed escapee, an industrial accident at a construction site with fatalities, or a multiple fatality vehicle accident, officers will be more effective as first responders if they know department procedures for handling these kinds of situations, chapter and verse. Without intimate knowledge of procedure, failure happens, and failure can make any cop look like the proverbial "dumb cop."

Even worse, when procedures aren't followed, the results can be disastrous. Officers or members of the public may suffer injury. Rescue and medical care may be delayed. Critical evidence can be lost, and violent offenders may even be released on technicalities. The officers involved could find themselves in court under cross examination because of a civil action that resulted from procedural break. That leaves supervisors and the department trying to explain why the officers were uninformed or unwilling to follow procedure—and that responsibility falls on the department.

Keeping Up to Date

Keeping up to date with policies and procedures is an ongoing effort essential to credible and consistent leadership. Police work has downtime, when calls for service are slow and all the work is caught up. Supervisors and mid-level managers need to take advantage of these breaks to review new directives but also to refresh themselves with details that may have faded a little. New court decisions regarding search and seizure could affect field interrogations and investigations. Changes to city, municipality, or state laws could determine if a summary arrest is appropriate. New departmental orders can affect daily operations. Any such changes should be shared with all members of a department verbally and in print. Supervisors should clearly convey their expectation for subordinates to be responsible and accountable in implementing them.

When changes are made and new orders are distributed to the department, supervisors should also take the time during roll calls to review them with the officers and explain how the changes will affect their operations.

In 1995, the District Court of Appeals for the District of Columbia handed down what became known as the "Douglas-Bay Decision." In brief, it said that it was illegal for police to make a warrantless entry into a potential defendant's apartment after another officer previously made a valid emergency search of the apartment for victims or someone involved in a shooting. In the Douglas-Bay case, the first officers on the scene had reason to enter the apartment and did so. They determined there was no evidence and left the premises.

Later, other officers and detectives arrived. They recovered evidence the first officers had missed, and it was used in the trial of the defendant. The defendant was found guilty. In the appeals trial, the evidence recovered by the second crew of police personnel was suppressed and the search was ruled illegal, and the conviction was overturned. The Douglas-Bay case was so significant that the DC Police put out a special order on the case with all its implications.[1] That way, if similar circumstances arose, officers would know how to handle the scene.

Within months of receiving that special order, patrol officers responded to a dispatched call for an unconscious person in a townhouse. They found a deceased man who had been shot several times. They searched the premises for other victims, witnesses, evidence that could be destroyed, and suspects. They found none, exited the property, and called for homicide and a police official to come to the townhouse.

At the time, I was a captain and the watch commander for my district, so I made my way to the townhouse. A couple of homicide detectives showed up a short time later, and we were briefed by the patrol officers who had entered the property. The homicide detectives called for the crime scene technicians to respond, and they proceeded to enter the townhouse.

As one of them reached for the doorknob, I cleared my throat. "You'll need a search warrant to enter," I said.

Predictably, being the prima donnas they were, we exchanged words. My words: "I am giving you a direct order to not enter those premises until you have a search warrant in hand signed by a judge—and I have seen it. Are we clear?"

The homicide detectives called the Criminal Investigations Division Watch Commander to the scene. The lieutenant conferred with the homicide detectives and then came to me. "A search warrant isn't necessary," he said crisply. "We're going in."

The back of my neck prickled. "The Douglas-Bay case decisions states—"

"I'm the CID Watch Commander," he snorted. "That's my decision."

I was bewildered. How could two homicide detectives and the CID Watch Commander be ignorant of a court decision that directly affected them?

Being the gentle soul that I am, I motioned for the lieutenant to step away from the others. We walked away from the patrol cars, and I began his education on accountability.

"How many bars are on a captain's insignia?" I asked.

"Two."

"How many bars on a lieutenant's insignia?"

"One," he said slowly. He clenched his jaw.

"Which is larger, two or one?"

"Two," he said stiffly.

"Do you know what it means to get a direct order from a superior officer?"

He took a deep breath and the color drained from his face. "I do."

"No one is to enter those premises until a search warrant is obtained. If anyone disobeys my direct order, he will be suspended. His police powers will be revoked pending formal disciplinary charges and a trial board hearing."

I conveyed my expectations in no uncertain terms—he would be held accountable for his actions. Would he repeat this error in judgment in the future? I didn't believe he would. The lieutenant was being held accountable in the performance of his sworn duty. As I stated earlier, the public has a legitimate expectation that officers know what they are doing and that what they are doing is lawful and in accordance with department orders. Further, I understood the need to be well-versed on written orders, giving me the ability to hold a subordinate accountable.

Why am I talking about operational accountability and responsibility? What does that have to do with creating an ethical police culture? Everything. You can't limit accountability and responsibility to just one facet of police duties and performance. If you do, you'll introduce confusion. Officers may believe they are virtuous in their performance of duty, using no excessive force or demeaning language. But if they don't put forth effort to protect and serve and perform operationally at a high level, they aren't actually following the principles of an ethical culture. Mediocre performance is not ethical. Review the core virtues—all of them in one way or another call on the police to protect and serve at the highest level. It is their responsibility.

A Career of Learning and Study

Police officials must be knowledgeable, current, well-informed, and literate about a department's written orders, court decisions, and the law. They are obliged to adopt a student mindset. Their career is one of learning and study. They owe it not only to the public but to their subordinates. Creating a culture of ethical conduct and holding subordinates accountable for their actions is essential, but a culture of high-performance expectation must be conveyed in all aspects of police service.

Fortunately, in the search warrant scenario just described, the only damage done was to police egos—along with considerable embarrassment. In less than ninety minutes, the homicide detectives returned with the search warrant.

The lesson is this: court decisions can fundamentally change standard operating procedures, making it imperative that police stay up to date on those decisions. Detectives and police officials are not immune from the requirement of career-long learning. Critically, court decisions give guidance on the use of force, both nonlethal and deadly. In 1985, the *Garner v. Tennessee* case set out strict guidelines for the use of deadly force by police officers. The decision raised several considerations. Is there a threat of serious physical harm to officers or others? If the suspect is fleeing, does the officer have probable cause to believe the suspect had been involved in an offense that caused or threatened serious bodily harm or death?

Some years later, in 1989, the *Graham v. Connor* case ruled that the police should consider the severity of the crime when using force, raising several other questions. Is the suspect an immediate threat? Is the suspect actively resisting arrest? Is the suspect attempting to evade arrest by flight?

The review of critical case law should be established by supervisors as a significant part of police culture. One must hold subordinates accountable and responsible to high police performance by following these and other rules. Failure to do so is, in fact, ethical misconduct. In such cases, police can be arrested and civil suits filed. When the police who swear to protect and serve the public are fired, the public no longer has faith in the agency. If first-line supervisors and mid-level managers are not knowledgeable and up to date, or if they don't have the moxie, they cannot adequately demand accountability from their subordinates. They cannot create and maintain a culture that has the trust and confidence of the public.

Corporals, sergeants, and lieutenants need to step up. Not only must they take responsibility for their own continual study, but they must also take every opportunity to train and update officers. Make training and updates a regular part of roll calls. Print posters to hang in the roll call room or locker rooms with bullet points that will catch officers' attention, something they can't miss. Produce pocket-sized, quick reference guides to hand out for officers to carry on duty.

When I started with the Metropolitan Police, seven probable cause misdemeanors existed. New ones were added periodically, and when I left, there were fifteen. Good to know and easy to put on a card for officers to carry. Some DC streets are only one or two blocks long, and remote, making the area complicated and tough to negotiate. Officers carried an information guide on their clipboard identifying every named, numbered, and lettered street in the area, with directions for how to get to it. Two messages are being conveyed. The first is the expectation that officers are literate in what they should do—when to press charges and how to get where they need to go. The second is that officers are literate in what they should not do—offer excuses for avoiding their duty. The overriding message is that all officers are accountable to possess the knowledge required to do the job.

Legislators in municipal, county, or state governments regularly change laws that directly affect police. During my many decades as a sworn police official, some laws shifted from criminal violations to civil violations, like littering, for example. Many new laws were enacted, such as those that protected the public from an increase in aggressive panhandling. The offense of vagrancy left the criminal code in 1972 after the US Supreme Court invalidated Jacksonville's vagrancy law as void. It was considered too vague. That invalidation sparked other changes to vagrancy laws across the country. The elements of some crimes—the actions that had to take place for it to be considered a criminal offense—were changed by legislators. For example, disorderly conduct was always a misdemeanor, but changes meant it was no longer a crime under disorderly conduct laws to direct obscenities at the police—a less-than-popular change among police officers.

Laws changed some felonies to misdemeanors, such as some drug offenses. Other changes moved misdemeanors up to felonies, such as carrying a pistol without a license. Some legislative action increased the number of criminal offenses that were probable cause misdemeanors, which meant an officer did not have to witness the action of the offense but could make the arrest based on probable cause. For example, let's say a police officer at the scene of a traffic accident finds one of the operators has a suspended driver's license. At one point in time, all an officer could do was write a ticket for operating on a suspended permit. When operating a vehicle without a license became a probable cause misdemeanor, the officer could summarily arrest that operator if sufficient facts led him to believe a crime had been committed. In this case, the driver of the other vehicle reported that the unlicensed driver had been behind the wheel at the time of the accident.

Informing Good Judgment

Most police service providers regularly update written orders, directives, policies, manuals, and other written documents. New procedures are published, and old ones are rescinded or replaced to keep police operations continually up to date. Changes such as these are generated for any number of reasons: new technologies like the issuance of body cams, political events causing changes in truancy enforcement, public demands leading to the recording of the race of an operator on all traffic stops, new tactics or strategies in the use of pepper spray for self-defense, new laws and court decisions as described, or the outcomes of civil litigation, such as those that caused prohibition of the choke hold neck restraint. These changes continually refine police operations to ensure ethical, professional, effective, legal, safe, and efficient service.

Clearly, failure to keep up to date and well-informed makes it difficult to build an ethics-based police culture. Without this culture, issues can arise when some aspects of policing are conveyed as important while others are not. If an ethical culture is to thrive with supervisor responsibility and subordinate accountability, it is necessary to also incorporate operational performance into every realm of police work.

Consider an officer who is on the scene of a domestic violence event. Many jurisdictions require a mandatory arrest in such situations. But in this case, the officer doesn't clearly understand all the elements of the crime, so they take no action. Is this an ethical issue? It can be argued either way, but shouldn't the officer be held responsible for inaction? Are officers not obliged to know what they are supposed to do and what they are not supposed to do?

In some regions, the policy on vehicle pursuit has changed. In some departments, officers are only permitted to initiate a vehicle pursuit related to a felony rather than just a traffic offense. Other departments prohibit vehicle pursuits unless it is in regard to a specific felony where serious bodily injury or the threat of serious bodily injury is involved. I'm confident that these changes were well publicized.

Every office and official should be well versed in vehicle pursuit policy. Simple? No. They must know which crimes are felonies and what elements of a crime determine it to be a felony. During my tenure with the city police, the District of Columbia Criminal Code contained three similar sounding crimes: Threats in a Menacing Manner, Threats to do Bodily Harm, and Threatening to Injure a Person. Only the latter was considered a felony. If officials didn't know the elements of each offense, and thus which was a felony, a vehicle pursuit may or may not have been authorized.

This may sound similar to the hypothetical scenario offered in chapter 5 to illustrate use of discretion. That example was loosely based on the true event that follows. In chapter 5, it was used to display officers' discretion. Here, in much more detail, it emphasizes the need to be well-versed and up to date on the rules. Even something as elementary as probable cause must be studied, reinforced, and hammered home continually.

Working as the "Night Hawk"—the acting chief of police—on one midnight tour, I responded to the location of a fatal traffic accident. The police district's watch commander informed me that a scout car officer was involved in an unauthorized pursuit that resulted in the fatal traffic accident. The operator of the vehicle being pursued had struck a utility pole and was dead on the scene. I told the officer involved in the pursuit to have a seat in my car, and then I asked him what had happened.

"I was dispatched to a sexual assault in progress," the officer said. He looked down, clearly shaken. "When I pulled up to the address, a woman came running out of the house, screaming, 'That's him! That's him!' She was wearing only a torn slip."

"What happened next?" I asked.

"I ordered the man to stop, but he ran to his car and sped off. I got into my vehicle, activated the emergency lights and sirens, and gave chase." The officer shook his head. "About eight or ten blocks later, he lost control and hit the pole."

I told the officer I would personally take a look at the whole sequence of events and that he would be treated fairly. I returned to the watch commander. "Why was that considered an unauthorized pursuit?"

The watch commander shrugged. "We interviewed the woman, and it was just a domestic."

No doubt charges would be placed against the officer. I decided to review the facts. After interviewing the woman, listening to the dispatch tapes, and talking to the officer again, I prepared my unsolicited report.

In my mind, the question was simple: Did the officer have probable cause to believe a felony had been committed that involved serious bodily injury or the threat of serious bodily injury? He did, and I articulated that in my report. He was dispatched to a sexual assault in progress and observed a woman in obvious distress, wearing only a torn slip. She was screaming, and she identified her alleged attacker. Add to that, the perpetrator failed to heed the officer's commands and fled the area in his vehicle.

Based on just those facts—the only facts presented to the officer— he had sufficient reason to believe a crime had been committed. He had probable cause to arrest the suspect had the suspect not crashed his car. Only later did he learn that there was no sexual assault in progress, and that it was in fact a domestic dispute. None of that information negated the facts and circumstances facing the officer at the time of his response.

My report of this incident stated that had the officer not engaged in the pursuit, based on the facts and circumstances he was presented with, he could have been charged with neglect of duty. The officer had probable cause to believe a felony had been committed that involved serious bodily injury or the threat of serious bodily injury. His pursuit was lawful and followed departmental guidelines.

No charges were filed. That watch commander, a mid-level manager, was ill-informed and just plain wrong, His failure to know what he should have known could have cost his subordinate dearly.

I relay this event as an example. Ignorance is *not* bliss. Superiors cannot hold subordinates accountable for not knowing what they should know if superiors don't know themselves. Perhaps worst is trying to hold subordinates accountable when they took the right action and you wrongly believe that they did not. That is culture shattering. The confidence and trust subordinates once had in their supervisor begins to deteriorate. It may not be visible outwardly, but internally they will question that supervisor's judgment. They may begin to question their decisions on other matters. The supervisor's legitimacy has taken a body blow. Don't let that happen. Dedicate some time to stay an expert on department rules, policies, laws, procedures, manuals and orders.

Some jurisdictions restrict vehicle pursuits unless there is probable cause, while others only need reasonable suspicion. Reasonable suspicion is less than probable cause but more than a hunch. It has to be based on "specific and articulable facts" taken together with "rational inferences from those facts," and your suspicion has to be associated with a specific person. Further, if you have reasonable suspicion that a person you detained is armed, you may pat the individual for weapons. Can you also search for drugs or other contraband based on reasonable suspicion? The rules say you cannot.

If supervisors take responsibility for building a strong ethical culture and hold their charges accountable for their actions, they must also build a strong operational culture. That takes highly specific knowledge. Continued learning is essential to effective operations. This pursuit is akin to what we expect of medical doctors. Throughout their careers, they test, acquire certifications, read medical journals, and stay current on new treatments, methods, and technologies. We expect nothing less than that from physicians. In policing, subordinates expect nothing less than that same dedication from their supervisors.

The public should not be served by uninformed and mediocre police officers who are supervised by uninformed and mediocre police officials any more than patients should be treated by uninformed and mediocre doctors. Both professions are afforded a great amount of discretion. Adequate use of that discretion depends upon a high level of continually updated knowledge. If the goal is to build a culture of ethical conduct based on the police core virtues, ignorance is unacceptable.

The books contain useful, important, and sometimes critical information, direction, guidelines, and much more. But every conceivable circumstance that police encounter cannot be included. Every single action they should and should not take is impossible to account for. Nonetheless, supervisors are responsible for demanding accountability. Applying the police core virtues and a solid knowledge of the books to any situation allows good judgment to inform action.

A patrol officer spends three hours of his tour of duty in the back room of a convenience store visiting with his girlfriend. Another officer goes off his assigned beat to take care of personal business. An hour before checkoff every night, an officer stops by his favorite bar and throws back three shooters. A young student needs three hundred copies of a flier for her school project, so her father, a police officer, takes care of it by using the police station copying machine. An officer reports for duty with no socks on. An officer talks on his personal cell phone while driving—even though it is a violation for the public to do so. Two officers get into a shoving and shouting match that almost comes to blows in the locker room. An officer shows up for roll with purple hair.

These are just a few examples of misconduct I have encountered, and I'm sure readers can easily come up with more. Every possible infraction cannot be written, but infractions they are, and they need addressing. Officers must be held accountable for these kinds of behaviors just as they are for ethical misconduct and violations of written directives. Without accountability for unwritten rules, ethical conduct and performance of duty are weakened.

Perhaps I should not use the term "unwritten rules"—"unwritten "infractions" probably works better. These infractions are not arbitrary and capricious. They are grounded in police core virtues of good judgment and trust—relating to public confidence in the police to protect and serve—as well as the responsibility to answer for your conduct and obligations.

In the absence of accountability for unwritten infractions, the three-legged milk stool will not stand. Leg one: adherence to the police core virtues. Leg two: adherence to departmental rules, regulations, and the law. Leg three: consequences—or accountability—for the unwritten infractions of officers doing what they are not supposed to or officers not doing what they are supposed to do.

I fear that the culture of high performance has taken a vacation in some police departments, or worse, left altogether. It is difficult to do the job under this most trying environment. First-line supervisors and mid-level managers must step in and step up. It's up to them to convey expectations for ethical performance of duty under all circumstances.

CONCLUSION

Change Is Within Reach

According to Mark Twain, "There are lies, damned lies, and statistics."
Some people believe that police cannot get their own house in
order—the station house, that is. From politicians, media outlets, academics, talking heads, and self-professed subject matter experts to the
general public, many people are convinced that the police have no business fixing anything. They are certain that *they* know what is best to
change a structure that most of them have no understanding of. (Read
more about this phenomenon in the appendix.)

Some of their solutions include the following: defunding the police; reducing police budgets; overloading operations with draconian
rules, policies, and directives; enacting new laws; and adding layers of
outside oversight.

Having noted this, I believe that some suggestions supported by
non–law enforcement individuals may actually be useful. The following
recommendations come from the Police Use of Force Project published
in 2016 by Campaign Zero.[1] The most interesting part about these recommendations is where they originated. Samuel Sinyangwe, a data sci-
entist and one of the cofounders of the organization, is developing strategies to end police violence. Sinyangwe's research has been thorough.

He examined the policies of ninety-four of the largest municipal
police departments in the United States and found that ethically per-

forming police departments outperform those that are not. In the list below, every recommendation—and he supports each one—was drawn from *existing* police polices:

1. Require officers to de-escalate before using force.
2. Use guidelines defining the types of force that can be used to respond to specific situations.
3. Restrict or ban choke holds and strangleholds.
4. Issue a verbal warning before using deadly force.
5. Prohibit officers from shooting at moving vehicles except in extreme circumstances.
6. Require officers to exhaust other options before resorting to deadly force.
7. Establish a duty for officers to intervene if one of their colleagues is using excessive force.
8. Require officers to report all uses of force or attempted use of force.

Let me repeat: departments with these requirements in place are ethically outperforming those who do not. Clearly, police departments have the ability to manage the use of excessive force and unethical behavior. But misleading information continues to garner public attention. Let's take a closer look at some of that information to find out what it really means.

At first glance, the numbers related to serious police offenses appear staggering. While use of excessive force and other unethical behavior should never occur, some of the numbers are deceptive. Consider a comment in USAFacts, reporting that "in 2015 roughly 996,000 people experienced force during their most recent police-initiated contact."[2] That's an outrageous number, but the article fails to differentiate between use of excessive force and the force that police are *legally* entitled to use, the minimum force *necessary* to diffuse myriad incidents or to protect themselves or others from harm.

With a similar lack of clarity, a *USA Today* report found that "at least 85,000 law enforcement officers across the USA have been investigated or disciplined for misconduct over the past decade."[3] That, too, sounds like a large number. But there are roughly 700,000 police in the United States. Investigating 85,000 officers over a ten-year period is equivalent to investigating just over 1 percent of all the officers in the United States per year. The operative word here is "investigated." Within the 1 percent investigated, the report fails to differentiate between those whose behavior is found to be acceptable and those who are ultimately disciplined. The results of an investigation can be unfounded, not sustained, or exonerated, meaning no discipline was deemed warranted. Only if the complaint is sustained would disciplinary action ensue. But even investigations with no proven merit were included in *USA Today*'s misleading report.

I was once the subject of an investigation for misconduct. While I was on patrol wearing full uniform and driving a marked car, a vehicle passed me traveling twenty miles per hour over the thirty-miles-per-hour speed limit in a major artery during rush hour. I conducted a traffic stop and issued the operator a speeding ticket. The vehicle operator filed a citizen's complaint against me, claiming she was issued the ticket just because she was female. She did not deny that she was speeding or that she passed me going twenty miles per hour over the limit. All citizens complaints are fully investigated, even frivolous ones, and this was no exception. It was found to be meritless.

If *USA Today* had separated investigations that resulted in discipline from those that did not, a clearer picture would emerge. Those 85,000 officers who were investigated, or 1 percent of the police force, would be reduced to a fraction of that amount.

How many other professions can withstand that kind of scrutiny? Here's some perspective. The *New England Journal of Medicine* reported that each year, 7.4 percent of all physicians had a malpractice claim filed against them. Of those claims, 1.6 percent resulted in a settlement.[4] That figure is higher than the percentage of investigations into police officer behavior, even *without* disregarding meritless inquiries.

These examples from USAFacts and *USA Today* are just a small sample of the "facts" that police force scrutiny is often based upon. Indeed, some statistics are gathered from reliable sources. They have credibility. Seldom are these resources cited widely, particularly by those who may have an agenda. In October 2018, the Bureau of Justice Statistics, the primary statistical agency of the Department of Justice, wrote, "Two percent of U.S. residents who had contact with police experienced threats or use of force." (2015) *Threat* of force isn't *use* of force. Eliminate the threat of force and instances of justified force from that cited 2 percent, and the actual use of excessive force is lower than the public is led to believe.

I cannot state this often enough: regardless of any discrepancy in statistics, no use of excessive force or unethical behavior should be tolerated. But the number of offenders is low, suggesting the problem is manageable in-house. Police departments don't need programs or regulations or budget pressure to implement change. They need the will and the know-how. That's what this book is for.

Police department executives may have little to say about what will come about from changes instituted by outside forces. They do, however, have a great deal of control over what happens inside. That is where change must begin—and with urgency. Only then will police agencies create the foundational shift required to recover from an unethical culture or build upon existing integrity.

The policies, procedures, general orders, and directives creating positive cultural change are evident. If they aren't already in place, they can be instituted. Creating an ethical police force culture is within reach. It is the responsibly of leadership to demand accountability from their charges. Ethics must be thoroughly rooted in police culture if we are to recover the trust and confidence of those we have sworn to serve and protect.

We can do this.

You can do this.

ACKNOWLEDGMENTS

My career as a police officer spans over four decades. I have seen much, worked with thousands, and served and protected many residents, neighborhoods and communities. From uniformed patrolman then detective to Deputy Chief of Police in Washington, DC, and, finally, Chief of Police for the Supreme Court of the United States, I always felt honored and relentlessly pursued excellence.

No list of acknowledgments could possibly recognize all of those I learned from, influenced me, and affected me profoundly. I would, however, be remiss if I did not acknowledge those individuals who have taken me to my station in life, resulting in my writing this book.

As a young boy and then a man, I was guided, taught, loved, and advised by one man: Merl E. Swope, my father. In his absence, my success would not be what it is. His police partner, Henry Stuart Heflin, became part of our family. His presence in my life for over fifty years provided enduring friendship and the sagest advice and solid consul.

In my pursuit of excellence, I discovered that constant learning was essential. I watched what others did, subordinates, peers, and superiors and became educated. The best of the best, the committed and dedicated influenced me. They were all brave, kind, empathetic, generous, and served the public and their subordinates at the highest level: Sergeant Rally Byrd, Sergeant Richard Barrow, Sergeant Jerry Pendry,

Sergeant Mark Houser, Lieutenant Eddie Lewis, Assistant Chief of Police Charles Samara, Roland Perry, Robert C. White, Al Broadbent, Chief of Police Sonia Proctor, Chief of Police William McManus, and Charles Ramsey.

I not only learned from watching, but also sought higher education and, in doing so, found educators who became friends. Their valued guidance, support, and teaching skills contributed significantly in my ability to write this book: professors Brian Forest and Emileo Viano.

It is quite impossible for me to articulate in this limited space the appreciation I hold for those I had the honor of growing up in the shadow of, as well as working with and learning from. These men and women enriched my life. It is because of them that I could not sit idle and do nothing while the policing profession became tarnished.

Special acknowledgments belong to Deborah Froese, my editor, who worked tirelessly with me in bringing this book to fruition. And Sandra Jonas, who, with her skills, knowledge, and valuable feedback, took me by the hand and led me through the maze of publishing that brought this work to print.

My sincere appreciation also to my friend and colleague Cathy Lanier, who wrote the foreword.

Lastly, I want to thank two of my closest friends of over fifty years. Tom Edmunds and David Crow, whose encouragement, contagious excitement, advice, and time drove me to the keyboard to put the words to paper. Without them in my corner, I would still be mulling over the first page.

APPENDIX

They Don't Know What
They Don't Know

It seems that many people have solutions to the state that police find themselves in. Academia, politicians, radical members of the public, those disenfranchised, and even ardent supporters of the police have something to say. But most of them are completely in the dark about police operations and police culture. Their "solutions" just won't solve the problem. Reducing the size or scope of a police department does nothing to reduce the use of excessive force.

While I wasn't allowed to join the academic club because I didn't have a PhD, I did manage to dip my toe into the waters of education as an adjunct professor at Johns Hopkins University and at the American University. Though I have respect for academia and friends at those institutions, I sometimes bring a different point of view. You can study a subject for decades and learn much about it, but until you are the *subject* of the study, any understanding will likely come up short.

Unfortunately, some people don't know what they don't know. This became clear to me after a quick perusal of suggested solutions from university experts. I was disappointed. They completely lacked an understanding of police operations.

Social contract theory states that individuals consent to surrender some of their freedoms and submit to the authority in exchange for protection of their remaining rights or maintenance of the social order.

Such a contract legitimizes the American system of government and the role of police in society. It should also inform law enforcement's attitude toward their occupation and the public. However, academia says officers have never read the Constitution, and few scholars or practitioners have defined which ethical principles should be taught and integrated into the profession. Wrangling over what to study is a mental exercise that doesn't help on the ground. Compared to the public, officers are experts on the laws of arrest, search, and seizure, whether they've read the Constitution or not, simply because those laws are critical to their work.

Although I know and concur with the concept of the social contract, social contract theory doesn't acknowledge on-the-ground circumstances. When a handcuffed prisoner stomps on the foot of the arresting officer, the officer's response won't be guided by social contract theory, even if it was studied at school or the police academy. If the officer is based in a police culture where police core virtues are alive and well and practiced, the officer will rely on prudence. Remember, prudence is self-discipline and self-control (see chapter 3). Their reaction will be determined by intellectual honesty rather than emotion. *Well, that was a damn dumb thing for me to do—getting so close he could stomp on my foot. His legs may have to be restrained.*

When I spoke about police core virtues at the Attorney General's National Symposium on Police Integrity in 1996, the LAPD listened. They determined those virtues were critical in their Rampart Division Corruption Report. Because the core virtues have been regarded with such respect and curiosity, I have written and published a number of articles about them. Since that time, social media has exploded with opinionated and generally ill-informed solutions to police brutality. News media participates in this gong show as well through interviews with so-called experts and various reports.

Brad Garrett, an ABC News opinion writer, explores a three-point plan to reduce police brutality[1]:

1. Test applicants for bias and the level of threat that will trigger an aggressive response.

2. Assess applicants for empathy and impulse control and do a background test.

3. Hold officers accountable for all unnecessary uses of force.

Although the ideas are good in principle, they are years away from implementation. To be effective, such tests must be valid and reliable, timely, and cost-effective. Even if a valid, reliable mechanism is developed, time and money will be major factors. It takes time for effective analysis, and the costs of recruiting officers and the selection process are already high. Potentially acceptable recruits are not knocking down the doors of police departments to join the ranks. Job fairs, advertising, and public vacancy announcements have time and financial costs associated with them as well, as discussed in chapter 6.

In one department I worked with, it took an average of twenty-five applicants to find one viable candidate at a cost of ten thousand dollars. Even then, there was no guarantee that the applicant would take the job if it were offered. Highly desirable candidates were typically in the running at multiple police departments. Hypothetically, even if all these approaches were effective, a rookie who landed in an unethical police culture with no accountability mechanisms in place would be indoctrinated into the strength and solidarity of that culture's power structure. Over time, that indoctrination risks eliminating any original benefits the most vigorous selection process would have found.

It is not the recruiting and selection procedure that is the major problem with the integrity of police officers, but the culture that new recruits find themselves in. That's where issues arise in the rotten barrel. This applies to their point of enhanced academy training also.

The third point in the plan put forth by ABC News—hold officers accountable for all unnecessary uses of force—is problematic. It will require taking on increasingly powerful police unions. Yes, police unions have a duty to defend all accused police officers. A union's defense does not guarantee the charged police officer won't be disciplined, and the process is costly for all parties. But if first-line supervisors and mid-level managers take the responsibility to hold officers accountable for their behavior, subordinates are held to a higher ethical standard. Fewer egregious incidents will require union intervention.

The online article "17 Solutions to Tackle Police Brutality in America" presents some good thoughts from Shaun King of the *New York Daily News* about wrestling with the problem, but unfortunately, King doesn't see the big picture behind some of his suggestions.[2] Let's take a look at these solutions to see where the problems lie and how the concepts align with the concept of ethics-based policing.

1. Radically diversify America's police departments.
This objective assumes that minority police officers won't engage with use of excessive force. I can say with certainty that this is not the case. Any officer, minority or otherwise, who enters a police culture without ethical reinforcement will become indoctrinated into that culture and behave accordingly.

All the police departments I am familiar with have already achieved racial diversity. In locations where minorities comprise a major portion of the constituency, minorities generally comprise the majority of the department. With roughly 18,000 police departments across the nation, there are some that may not.

2. Require American police to have more training than cosmetologists.
This solution suggests police require more education than simply academy training. The thing is, they're already getting it. Police are assigned to a senior veteran officer for on-the-job training that can last several months and include written evaluations by the senior officer. Many departments have in-service training presented at roll calls each week, and still others require periodic forty-hour courses for veteran officers. Departments offer in-house training. They pay for external training on a plethora of subjects. Higher education is subsidized by many departments.

3. Police must be routinely and randomly tested for steroids and other illegal drugs.
Agreed. Drug use by a police officer could impair judgment, performance, and behavior. It is worse if it is addictive or a criminal violation to possess. This solution was standard operating procedure during my tenure.

4. Bad apples must be fired.
Agreed.

5. Police must be required to earn four-year degrees.
Education is commendable and desirable, but that also limits the applicant pool. If one objective is to diversify an agency, a four-year degree will, unfortunately, impose more challenges. A minority college graduate has many options other than police work. Another factor, in my experience, is that the attrition rate for college graduates is higher.

6. Policing for profit must become a banned practice. A profit motive must never undergird law enforcement.
But civil forfeiture is legal and useful tool. I have seized property for civil forfeiture, but my personal view was never that I or my department would benefit from it. Further, that was the also view of those I served with.

7. We must overhaul 911—particularly for mental-health-related calls. It is the rotary phone of emergency services.
The call number 911 is badly in need of modernization. Coordination with responders specially trained to deal with the mentally ill is helpful, and I've had the opportunity to call social services for situations involving the mentally ill. Unfortunately, their responses, even during business hours, aren't timely. Creating an efficient and effective 24/7 mental health emergency response system will take concentrated effort at a considerable cost. If put into effect, it could provide a trained re-

source available to police officers to call upon when needed, just as in a medical emergency, they can call an ambulance with trained responders. Police are trained in a myriad of skills and learn much through experience. They are taught first aid, but they are ill-equipped to address very serious physical health emergencies. Similarly, when interacting with an individual experiencing critical mental health issues, a specialist with advanced skills would be beneficial to all.

8. Take women from 12 percent of the police force to 50 percent—they are more professional, less brutal, and just as effective.

Although this suggestion comes without empirical evidence, my experience tells me that they are correct. However qualified women may be, police work is not a profession many women seek. Personally, I've vigorously recruited women for police positions, and it's extremely challenging. Perhaps Shaun King isn't aware of that difficulty.

9. Require cops to live in or near the areas they police.

This sounds great if you are under the impression that living where you work will reduce brutality. Although it may be easier for unethical officers to mistreat strangers than friends or acquaintances, I'm unaware of any study that links fewer incidents of brutality with a residency requirement. Cops want what most people want: a safe community and good schools. Residency requirements thwarts that. Add that to the demand for increased minorities and women on the force, and the applicant pool grows even smaller. There were no residency requirements during my career, and the ethical culture I worked in virtually eliminated use of excessive force.

10. Communities of color actually need less policing.

Shaun King would have benefited from attending one of the literally hundreds of community meetings I held with residents of minority communities. Never once was the notion of less policing broached. In fact, law-abiding citizens always asked for more. Proven successful interventions like problem-oriented policing would not fit with a solution of less policing. Communities of color just want to be protected and served like everyone else.

11. American police must be regularly tested for racial bias.
This theoretically good idea is challenged by finding valid and reliable precision testing and how to pay for it. Good luck with that. A one-hour talk with a psychiatrist for an applicant screening, including a written report, comes with a price tag of $800. If a valid, reliable test were developed and a department tested 250 officers once every five years at a cost of $800 each, it would cost that department $400,000 a year for testing alone. That doesn't include the cost covering an officer's time when that officer is out of service to take the test. A much simpler approach is the development of an ethical culture where racial bias would be completely unacceptable.

12. America police must be regularly tested and treated for PTSD.
This, too, is a good idea in principle. Just like testing for bias, a valid, reliable test would be required and come with significant costs. Accuracy is an issue. What happens to an officer who fails either this PTSD test or the racial bias test described in number 11, yet has never exhibited any forms of racial bias or shown any symptoms of PTSD?

13. Why we must take bad laws on policing all the way to the Supreme Court.
Jurisdiction legislators make the laws, not the police. Shaun King suggests bypassing the legislative process and letting the courts make the laws. But the courts aren't on the ground, and they aren't fully informed—they don't know what they don't know. As a result, their decision-making ability is impaired.

Take a look at open-air drug markets. I spent most of my career in low socioeconomic minority neighborhoods, some debilitated by street sales of marijuana, twenty-four hours a day, seven days a week, month after month. I know, it is just marijuana, a mild drug. What harm could there be? But these neighborhoods were flooded with social and physical disorder, increased crimes, and heightened fear of crime. Still, to an outside observer, it was just marijuana.

During community meetings, residents expressed desperation for the state of their community. They needed the help of the police. I provided that help. Dealers were arrested for possession of marijuana with intent to distribute, for the sale of marijuana, and for possession of marijuana while armed. These offenses were generally pleaded down to misdemeanors, creating only a minor inconvenience to the dealers and sellers.

During that time, the United States Attorney for the District of Columbia initiated a pilot program in my police district. This program was called Community Prosecution—another name for Community Policing. Two assistant US attorneys were assigned and housed at the station. Of course, I brought these attorneys to community meetings so they could hear for themselves how neighborhoods were affected. I gave them a first-rate education on the open-air drug markets and their impact on the folks we—the police and the prosecutors—were sworn to protect. They were shocked. Prosecutors began to see things differently. Eventually, open-air drug markets were closed and some of these neighborhoods improved. So, if you don't live there and suffer, be careful what laws you may wish to "fix." The legislative process is the mechanism for changing laws, not the judiciary. People and their votes advocate for the laws they want or do not want by electing individuals that work for them.

14. Good police officers must actually speak out on bad cops.
As this book has shown, speaking out is an intrinsic part of ethics-based policing.

15. We must decriminalize mental illness.
Where is mental illness a criminal offense? Police can involuntarily admit someone to a mental health facility only if the individual is a threat to themselves or to others. Perhaps Shaun King, as recommended in the full text of this point, should have said the police need much more

training in dealing with those with mental illness. I am a firm believer in any training that improves officers' efficacy in their interactions with the mentally ill.

16. We need to unleash the full power of body cameras.
If the community sees utility in body cameras, they should be used. Barak Ariel, a researcher who has studied the effectiveness of police body cameras, offers these words of advice: "While the variability in the effectiveness of these cameras is disappointing, perhaps it shouldn't be so surprising. After all, what could work for a sheriff's department in Iowa may not necessarily apply to other places."[3]

So even though Ariel is a great supporter of body cams, he advises police departments to move slowly and thoughtfully in their adoption. "There are certainly a lot of issues to address." He also adds that there are still plenty of technological hurdles.

In a 2018 article, the National Institute of Justice states, "Current research suggests that body-worn cameras may offer benefits for law enforcement. However, additional research is needed to understand the value of the technology for the field."[4]

And in a 2019 article for the online news and opinion outlet, *Medium*, Delonte Harrod writes:

> Police officers have turned off body cameras during routine stops; some police departments have made it difficult for citizens to gain access to body camera footage; body cameras distort images; the wearer is off-screen with the suspects or civilians as the dominant actors; and the shaky, low quality of body cam footage often adds to deceptive intensity, which help justify police use of force.[5]

17. Police departments must create and enforce reasonable new use of force standards.
Many departments already have reasonable use of force standards, as found by the Use of Force Project, mentioned earlier. Those that do not

should create them as a necessary component of an ethical police culture where the sergeants and lieutenants do the enforcing. No ethical culture, little enforcement.

While numerous ideas and recommendations for the improvement of policing in the United States are being circulated, too many of the people circulating them don't know what they don't know. Some of the suggestions are good. Some are even viable. Unfortunately, many of them are easily voiced but difficult or impossible to implement and do little to create beneficial long-term impacts. The only clear way forward is to create a strong foundation that not only supports but also encourages and reinforces ethics-based policing.

NOTES

INTRODUCTION: The Time for Change Is Now

1. Brad Garrett, "A 3-Point Plan to Help Reduce Police Brutality and Make Cops Better: Opinion," ABC News , June 12, 2020, https://abcnews.go.com/US/point-plan-reduce-police-brutality-make-cops-column/story?id=71195570.

2. Timothy Roufa, "What to Know about the Psychological Screening for Police Officers," LiveAbout, updated August 4, 2019, https://www.liveabout.com/psychological-exams-and-screening-for-police-officers-974785.

3. Roufa, "What to Know."

4. DeRay McKesson et al., *Police Use of Force Policy Analysis*, September 20, 2016, https://8cantwait.org/files/police-use-of-force-report.pdf.

5. Emily Leayman, "Alexandria Police Compare Crime Data from 2019 and 2020," Patch, October 5, 2020, https://patch.com/virginia/oldtownalexandria/alexandria-police-compare-crime-data-2019-2020.

6. WTVM, "Comparing Crime Trends in Columbus from 2019 to 2020," WTVM, updated August 28, 2020, https://www.wtvm.com/2020/08/28/comparing-crime-trends-columbus/.

7. "NYPD Announces Citywide Crime Statistics for June 2020," New York City Police Department, press release, July 6, 2020, https://www1.nyc.gov/site/nypd/news/pr0706/nypd-citywide-crime-statistics-june-2020.

8. Rocco Parascandola, " 'Blue Flight' Retirements Thinning NYPD Ranks to Levels Not Seen in Nearly a Decade," *New York Daily News*, October 8, 2020, https://www.nydailynews.com/new-york/nyc -crime/ny-nypd-retirements-surge-20201008-gh5yzwbgz5dgfh4h mvvys6eur4-story.html.

9. I mention the LAPD because they made this disclosure public, but others did not, so they will remain confidential.

ONE: Bad Apples or Bad Barrel?

1. Daniel Villarreal, "More Than 1,000 Black Lives Matter Protesters Harmed by Police As Public Support for Racial Justice Movement Decreases," *Newsweek*, October 29, 2020, https://www.newsweek. com/more-1000-black-lives-matter-protesters-harmed-police-public -support-racial-justice-movement-1543410.

2. John Kelly and Mark Nichols, "We Found 85,000 Cops Who've Been Investigated for Misconduct. Now You Can Read Their Records," *USA Today News*, updated June 11, 2020, https://www.usatoday .com/in-depth/news/investigations/2019/04/24/usa-today-revealing -misconduct-records-police-cops/3223984002/.

3. FindLaw Staff, reviewed by Kellie Pantekoek, "Excessive Force and Police Brutality," FindLaw, updated June 2, 2020, https://www .findlaw.com/criminal/criminal-procedure/excessive-force-and-police -brutality.html.

4. Bernard C. Parks, *Los Angeles Police Department Board of Inquiry into the Rampart Area Corruption Incident: Public Report*, March 1, 2000, i–ii. (Online version available at https://lapdonlinestrgeacc.blob .core.usgovcloudapi.net/lapdonlinemedia/2022/02/Rampart-Area -Corruption.pdf.)

5. Gerald W. Lynch, ed., *Human Dignity and the Police: Ethics and Integrity in Police Work* (Springfield: Charles C. Thomas, 1999), 115.

6. Lynch, *Human Dignity*, 115.

7. Michael J. Palmiotto, ed., *Police Misconduct: A Reader for the 21st Century* (Upper Saddle River , NJ: Prentice Hall, 2001), 118–19.

8. Lynch, *Human Dignity*, 115.

9. Palmiotto, *Police Misconduct*, 120–22.

10. David Burnham, "Police in Philadelphia Called Corrupt; Panel Says Rizzo Tried to Bar Inquiry," *New York Times*, March 11, 1974, 1. (Online version available at https://www.nytimes.com/1974/03/11

/archives/police-in-philadelphia-called-corrupt-panel-says-rizzo-tried
-to-bar.html.)

11. Michael J. Palmiotto, *Police Misconduct*, 139–42.

12. Paul Keegan, "The Thinnest Blue Line," *New York Times Magazine*,
    March 31, 1996, 32–35.

13. Michael J. Palmiotto, *Police Misconduct*, 38–39.

14. *Report of the Independent Commission on the Los Angeles Police Depart-*
    ment, 1991, iii–iv, 31. (Online version available at https://michel
    lawyers.com/wp-content/uploads/2010/06/Report-of-the-Independent
    -Commission-on-the-LAPD-re-Rodney-King_Reduced.pdf.)

15. Melorie Begay, "Lawsuit Claims Springfield, Oregon, Police Violated
    Protesters' Civil Rights," OPB, March 9, 2021, www.opb.org/article
    /2021/03/09/lawsuit-black-lives-matter-protests-springfield-oregon
    -police-civil-rights/.

16. Steering Law Firm, "California Police Misconduct Lawsuits, Awards,
    and Settlements," Law Offices of Jerry L. Steering, accessed April 9,
    2021, http://steeringlaw.com/police-misconduct-and-other-civil-rights
    -case-results/.

17. The term "Brady Cop" arose from the Brady disclosure rule. Estab-
    lished by the United States Supreme Court in *Brady v. Maryland*
    (1963), this rule requires the prosecution to turn over to the defense
    attorney any evidence that may exonerate the defendant—including
    any evidence of unethical behavior by police officers involved, which
    would then attest to their lack of integrity.

18. J. Thomas Wren, *The Leader's Companion: Insights on Leadership*
    Through the Ages (New York: The Free Press, 1995), 493, Kindle.

TWO: The Ethical Gatekeeper

1. J. K. Anderson, *Military Theory and Practice in the Age of Xenophon*
   (Berkeley: University of California Press, 1970), 75.

FOUR: Authority, Power, and Discretion

1. Egon Bittner, *The Functions of the Police in Modern Society: A Review*
   of Background Factors, Current Practices, and Possible Role Models, National Institute of Mental Health, Center for Studies of Crime and
   Delinquency, Public Health Service Publication No. 2059 (Washington, DC: Government Printing Office, 1970), 46.

2. Egon Bittner was a sociologist known for his groundbreaking studies
   of relationships between police and society. His most notable work is

The Functions of the Police in Modern Society (1970), in which he argues that the police are defined by their capacity to use force. Other significant works include *Aspects of Police Work* (1990), "The Capacity to Use Force as the Core of the Police Role" (essay in *Moral Issues in Police Work*, Frederick Elliston and Michael Feldberg, eds., 1985), and "The Police on Skid-Row: A Study of Peace Keeping" (article in *American Sociological Review*, October, 1967), where he presented police discretion as a necessary and positive police attribute.

FIVE: Corruption and the Noble Cause

1. Keya Vakil, "The 'Warrior Mindset' of Cops Is One of the Biggest Obstacles to Police Reform," *Courier*, June 18, 2020, https://archive .couriernewsroom.com/2020/06/16/police-culture-blocks-reform/.
2. Seth Stoughton, "Law Enforcement's 'Warrior' Problem," *Harvard Law Review Forum*, April 10, 2015, https://harvardlawreview .org/2015/04/law-enforcements-warrior-problem/.
3. Egon Bittner, *The Functions of the Police in Modern Society: A Review of Background Factors, Current Practices, and Possible Role Models*, National Institute of Mental Health, Center for Studies of Crime and Delinquency, Public Health Service Publication No. 2059 (Washington, DC: Government Printing Office, 1970), 46.
4. US Attorney's Office, "FBI Agent Pleads Guilty to Federal Corruption Charges, Admitting He Attempted to Improperly Influence Criminal Case," FBI Los Angeles, press release, March 23, 2009, https:// archives.fbi.gov/archives/losangeles/press-releases/2009/la032309.htm.
5. Michelle McPhee, "'Whitey' Bulger Trial Details FBI Corruption," ABC News, June 27, 2013, https://abcnews.go.com/US/whitey -bulger-trial-details-fbi-corruption/story?id=19510081.

SIX: Synergy in the Police Force

1. These observations were raised during a facilitated conversation I took part in.
2. Bernard C. Parks, *Los Angeles Police Department Board of Inquiry into the Rampart Area Corruption Incident: Public Report*, March 1, 2000, ii. (Online version available at https://lapdonlinestrgeacc.blob.core.us govcloudapi.net/lapdonlinemedia/2022/02/Rampart-Area-Corrup tion.pdf.)
3. Timothy Roufa, "What to Know about the Psychological Screening for Police Officers," LiveAbout, updated August 4, 2019, https://

www.liveabout.com/psychological-exams-and-screening-for-police
-officers-974785.

EIGHT: Conveying Expectations

1. J. Sterling Livingston, "Pygmalion in Management," *Harvard Business Review*, January 2003. (Online version available at https://hbr.org /2003/01/pygmalion-in-management.)

2. "Biography: Jaime Escalante," Biography (website), accessed December 19, 2020, https://www.biography.com/scholar/jaime-escalante. Escalante's story was portrayed in the 1988 film *Stand and Deliver* starring Edward James Olmos.

NINE: Mentoring First-Line Supervisors

1. Mary Abbajay, "Mentoring Matters: Three Essential Elements of Success," *Forbes*, January 20, 2019, https://www.forbes.com/sites/mary abbajay/2019/01/20/mentoring-matters-three-essential-element-of -success/?sh=533885f445a9.

TEN: Credible and Consistent Leadership

1. A special order is a memorandum of significant importance that requires immediate printing and distribution among all members of the department to institute immediate change. It becomes a permanent document in the department's general orders (policies and procedures).

CONCLUSION: Change Is Within Reach

1. DeRay McKesson et al., *Police Use of Force Policy Analysis*, September 20, 2016, https://8cantwait.org/files/police-use-of-force-report.pdf. For more information on how Campaign Zero is affecting ethical policing, see the introduction and chapter 1.

2. "Measuring What Matters: Addressing Police Reform Must Start with Accurate Data," USAFacts, updated September 23, 2020, https:// usafacts.org/articles/measuring-what-matters-addressing-police-reform -must-start-accurate-data/.

3. John Kelly and Mark Nichols, "We Found 85,000 Cops Who've Been Investigated for Misconduct. Now You Can Read Their Records," *USA Today News*, updated June 11, 2020, https://www.usatoday .com/in-depth/news/investigations/2019/04/24/usa-today-revealing -misconduct-records-police-cops/3223984002/.

4. Anupam B. Jena, et al., "Malpractice Risk According to Physician Specialty," *New England Journal of Medicine* 365 (August 18, 2011), https://www.nejm.org/doi/full/10.1056/nejmsa1012370.

APPENDIX: They Don't Know What They Don't Know

1. Brad Garrett, "A 3-Point Plan to Help Reduce Police Brutality and Make Cops Better: Opinion," ABC News, June 12, 2020, https://abc-news.go.com/US/point-plan-reduce-police-brutality-make-cops-column/story?id=71195570.

2. Luke Miller, "17 Solutions to Tackle Police Brutality in America," Truth Theory, August 24, 2016, https://truththeory.com/17-solutions-to-tackle-police-brutality-in-america/.

3. Barak Ariel, "Do Police Body Cameras Really Work?" *IEEE Spectrum*, May 4, 2016, https://spectrum.ieee.org/consumer-electronics/portable-devices/do-police-body-cameras-really-work.

4. Brett Chapman, "Body-Worn Cameras: What the Evidence Tells Us," National Institute of Justice, November 14, 2018, https://nij.ojp.gov/topics/articles/body-worn-cameras-what-evidence-tells-us.

5. Delonte Harrod, "Are Police Body Cameras Effective?" Medium, October 14, 2019, https://medium.com/the-intersection/do-police-body-cameras-work-2d0b89c1cffe.

INDEX

Note: Page numbers followed by "n" refer to notes.

classroom approaches to training,
89–91
class schedule, training, 93
coaching and mentoring, 113–20
  as an ongoing process, 120
  benefits of, 114–15
  encouraging skill application,
  118–19
  expressing concern, 119
  facilitating learning, 117–18
  feedback, 118
  functions, 114
  identifying needs, 116–17
  recognition and praise, 119–20
  time, 120
  verifying success, 119
Code Enforcement, xx
code of ethics, 16, 72
commendations. See recognition/
  commendations/rewards
communication of expectations. See
  expectations
communities of color, 146–47
Community Prosecution, 148
community trust. See trust
concerns, expressing, 119
Constitution, 9, 52, 60, 111, 142
core virtues, 15, 28–29, 39–40, 53,
  142
  bell curve, 44–51
  performing duty with, 56–57
  as standard operating procedures
  (SOPs), 51
  training program, 92
corruption
  cure/solution, 8–10
  investigations, 3–4
  Lexow Commission, 7
  noble cause, 59–74

corruption (continued)
  publicized examples, 6–8
  responding effectively to,
  10–15
  teaching risks of, 59–60
counseling and career-facilitation
  function of mentoring, 114
courage, xxiii, 15, 28, 33, 41–42,
  104
Courier, 65
criminal investigations
  noble cause and, 69–74
  perception, 70
  See also detectives
criminal justice system, 7
cultural diversity training, xxi
culture
  ethical (see ethical culture)
  as source of problems, 5
  supervision, 5–6
  unethical, 9
Curran Committee, 7

Declaration of Independence, 52
defensive tactics, 65
Department of Justice, 3, 138
detectives, 69–74
  performance evaluations, 73–74
  responsibility, 69
  selection, 72–73
  unethical acts, 69
Dirty Harry, 63–65
disciplinary actions/measures, xxiv,
  14
discretion, 53, 54
  ethical implications, 54, 57
  scenarios, 54–58
diversity, 9, 144
documentation, 111–12

ABOUT THE AUTHOR

ROSS SWOPE grew up in the world of law enforcement. The son of a cop, he joined the Washington, DC, police force soon after he graduated from the University of Maryland in 1972. Over the next forty-three years, he rose through the ranks, ultimately becoming deputy chief of the DC Metropolitan Police Department and then the chief of police of the US Supreme Court.

A highly effective law enforcement manager and forward thinker, he pursued continuing education and applied it to every department he served. In addition to his numerous awards and commendations, he holds three master's degrees—applied behavioral science; justice, law, and society; and applied criminology—making him the most highly decorated and educated police official in the DC Metropolitan Police Department when he retired.

Swope has been published locally, nationally, and internationally on such topics as community policing, problem-oriented policing, leadership issues, and effective policing strategies. Generally recognized as the creator and author of the seminal work on police ethics, he has been widely cited in major publications on that subject.

Also an avid outdoorsman, Swope has had his writing and photography featured in adventure magazines. He lives in Gambrills, Maryland.

Made in United States
Orlando, FL
07 October 2024

52437112R00118